The Complete Christmas Fudge Cookbook

Quick, Easy and Delicious Christmas Fudge Recipes with a Modern Twist and Delicious Traditions

BY: LINDA L. KENNEDY

TABLE OF CONTENTS

Quick, Easy and Delicious Christmas Fudge Recipes with a Modern Twist and Delicious Traditions...................................i

1.Red Velvet Fudge 5

2.Salted Caramel Fudge 5

3.Maple Walnut Fudge.......................................5

4.Mocha Almond Fudge 6

5.Pecan Pie Fudge 6

6.Eggnog Fudge 6

7.Candy Cane Fudge 7

8.Oreo Fudge 7

9.Classic Chocolate Fudge 7

10.Peppermint Bark Fudge 7

11.White Chocolate Cranberry Fudge................8

12.Gingerbread Fudge 8

13.Toffee Crunch Fudge.....................................8

14.Peppermint Mocha Fudge 9

15.Cinnamon Roll Fudge 9

16.Cherry Almond Fudge 9

17.Pumpkin Spice Fudge 9

18.Butterscotch Pecan Fudge 10

19.Caramel Apple Fudge:...................................10

20.Peanut Butter Cup of Fudge: 10

21.Chocolate Chip Cookie Dough Fudge:...........10

22.White Chocolate Peppermint Fudge:.............11

23.Marshmlet Swirl Fudge 11

24.Coconut Macaroon Fudge..............................11

24.Salted Pretzel Fudge 11

25.Cranberry Orange Fudge...............................11

26.Rocky Road Fudge...12

27.Snickerdoodle Fudge.....................................12

28.Chocolate Orange Fudge................................12

29.Nutella Swirl Fudge 13

30.Cookies and Cream Fudge..............................13

31.White Chocolate Raspberry Fudge 13

32.Peanut Butter and Jelly Fudge 14

33.S'mores Fudge...14

34.White Chocolate Cinnamon Fudge 14

35.Hazelnut Chocolate Fudge 15

36.Raspberry Cheesecake Fudge 15

37.Hot Cocoa Fudge...15

38.Andes Mint Fudge 16

39.Tiramisu Fudge..16

40.Key Lime Pie Fudge 16

41.Lemon Blueberry Fudge.................................17

42.Cranberry Pistachio Fudge............................17

43.Mint Chocolate Swirl Fudge 17

44.Caramel Popcorn Fudge:................................18

45.Mocha Peppermint Fudge: 18

46.Coconut Lime Fudge: 18

47.Red Hot Cinnamon Fudge: 19

48.Chai Spice Fudge 19

49.Pistachio Cranberry Fudge 19

50.Sugar Cookie Fudge.......................................20

51.Buttermint Fudge...20

52.Chocolate Covered Strawberry Fudge 20

53.Brownie Batter Fudge 21

54.Maple Bacon Fudge 21

55.Almond Joyful Fudge......................................21

56.Caramel Macchiato Fudge 22

57.Pineapple Coconut Fudge 22

58. Pumpkin Pecan Fudge...................................22

59. Bourbon Pecan Pie Fudge 23

60. Chocolate Hazelnut Fudge 23

61.Dark Chocolate Cherry Fudge 23

62.Ginger Snap Fudge 23

63.Almond Maple Fudge.....................................24

64.Chocolate Covered Pretzel Fudge 24

65.Cherry Chocolate Chunk Fudge.....................24

66.Toffee Almond Fudge.....................................25

67.S'mores Marshmlet Fudge.............................25

68.Apple Pie Fudge 25

69.White Chocolate Toffee Fudge 26

70.Churro Fudge 26

71.Fig and Walnut Fudge 26

72.Raspberry Almond Fudge.................................27

73.Strawberry Shortcake Fudge:...........................27

74.Peppermint Oreo Fudge: 27

75.Chocolate Coconut Almond Fudge: 28

76.Maple Cinnamon Pecan Fudge: 28

77.Caramel Banana Fudge 28

78.Nutty Irishman Fudge 28

79.Blueberry Cheesecake Fudge 29

80.Cinnamon Pecan Fudge 29

81.White Chocolate Apricot Fudge 29

82.Cookies and Creme Fudge 30

83.Cranberry Eggnog Fudge...................................30

84.Pomegranate Pistachio Fudge 30

85.Raspberry Lemonade Fudge 31

86.Toffee Brownie Fudge.......................................31

87.Blueberry Lemon Fudge....................................31

88.Pecan Praline Fudge..31

89.M&M Cookie Fudge 32

90.Chocolate Malt Fudge.......................................32

91.White Chocolate Pistachio Cranberry Fudge 32

92.Butterscotch Chocolate Swirl Fudge 33

93.Black Forest Fudge:...33

94.Pina Colada Fudge:..33

95.Cappuccino Fudge:..34

96.White Chocolate Cherry Fudge:........................34

97.Peppermint Hot Chocolate Fudge:....................34

98.Chocolate Pistachio Fudge:...............................34

99.Turtle Pecan Fudge:..35

100.Chocolate Cherry Cordial Fudge: 35

101.Black and White Fudge 36

102.Peanut Butter Banana Fudge 36

103.Pumpkin Spice Latte Fudge 36

104.Lemon Poppy Seed Fudge...............................37

105.Hazelnut Espresso Fudge.................................37

106. Apple Cinnamon Fudge 37

107.Salted Caramel Pretzel Fudge 38

108. Maple Bacon Pancake Fudge 38

109. Raspberry Truffle Fudge..............................38

110.Chocolate Marshmlet Swirl Fudge 38

111.Blueberry Almond Fudge 39

112.White Chocolate Strawberry Fudge 39

113.Almond Joy Brownie Fudge 39

114.Banana Nut Bread Fudge 39

115.Mint Oreo Cookie Fudge 40

116.Coconut Chocolate Swirl Fudge 40

117. Almond Joy Cheesecake Fudge 40

118. Chocolate Raspberry Cheesecake Fudge 41

119. Irish Cream Coffee Fudge...............................41

120.Dark Chocolate Mint Fudge:...........................41

121.S'mores Marshmlet Swirl Fudge: 41

122.Peanut Butter and Jelly Swirl Fudge: 42

123.Hazelnut Cherry Fudge: 42

124.Almond Raspberry Swirl Fudge 42

125.Ginger Lemon Fudge 43

126. Espresso Chocolate Swirl Fudge 43

127. Eggnog Cookie Fudge 43

128.Almond Cherry Fudge 44

129.Cranberry White Chocolate Swirl Fudge 44

130.Chocolate Hazelnut Swirl Fudge 44

131.Chocolate Pistachio Raspberry Fudge.....................44

132.Tiramisu Cheesecake Fudge.......................45

133. Salted Caramel Apple Pie Fudge 45

134.Cinnamon Roll Cheesecake Fudge 45

135.Pecan Pie Cheesecake Fudge 46

136.Butterscotch Pecan Cookie Fudge 46

137.Chocolate Cherry Almond Fudge 46

138.Pumpkin Praline Fudge 47

139.White Chocolate Almond Joy Fudge 47

140.Caramel Apple Cider Fudge.............................47

141.Peppermint Mocha Cheesecake Fudge....................48

142.Caramel Brownie Cheesecake Fudge 48

143.Chocolate Raspberry Truffle Fudge....................48

144.Gingerbread Cheesecake Fudge 48

145.White Chocolate Eggnog Fudge 49

146.Cranberry Stuffed Acorn Squash...............49

147.Pecan Pie Bars...50

148.Mexican Churros with Chocolate Sauce....................50

149.Polish Bigos (Hunter's Stew) 50

150.Turkish Lahmacun 51

RECIPES

1.Red Velvet Fudge

Prep Time: 15 mins

Cook Time: 10 mins

Total Time: 25 mins

Servings: 16 pieces

Ingredients:

- 2 cups of white chocolate chips
- 1 14-oz can sweetened condensed milk
- 1 tsp vanilla extract
- 2 tbsp unsweetened cocoa powder
- 2 tbsp red food coloring
- 1/2 cup of chop-up pecans (non-compulsory)

Instructions:

1. Leave enough parchment paper hanging over the sides of an 8x8-inch square baking pan to get the baked goods out without damaging the pan.
2. Add white chocolate chips and sweetened condensed milk to a medium saucepan and stir up to smooth. Stirring constantly, melt the chocolate in a saucepan over low heat up to it is completely smooth.
3. Turn off the heat and whisk in the chocolate powder, vanilla essence, and red food coloring.
4. Add some chop-up pecans if you like.
5. Spread the Mixture evenly in the pan after pouring the Mixture in.
6. Fudge Must be chilled in the fridge for at least two hrs, or up to firm.
7. When the fudge has set, take it out of the pan by the parchment paper overhangs. Serve by slicing into squares.

Nutrition (per serving):

Cals: 212, Fat: 10g, Carbs: 27g

Protein: 3g

2.Salted Caramel Fudge

Prep Time: 10 mins

Cook Time: 10 mins

Total Time: 20 mins

Servings: 16 pieces

Ingredients:

- 2 cups of white chocolate chips
- 1 14-oz can sweetened condensed milk
- 1/2 cup of caramel sauce
- 1/2 tsp sea salt
- 1 tsp vanilla extract

Instructions:

1. Leave enough parchment paper hanging over the sides of an 8x8-inch square baking pan to get the baked goods out without damaging the pan.
2. Add white chocolate chips and sweetened condensed milk to a medium saucepan and stir up to smooth. Stirring constantly, melt the chocolate in a saucepan over low heat up to it is completely smooth.
3. Combine the caramel sauce, salt, and vanilla by stirring them together.
4. Spread the Mixture evenly in the pan after pouring the Mixture in.
5. Fudge Must be chilled in the fridge for at least two hrs, or up to firm.
6. When the fudge has set, take it out of the pan by the parchment paper overhangs. Serve by slicing into squares.

Nutrition (per serving):

Cals: 202, Fat: 8g

Carbs: 31g, Protein: 3g

3.Maple Walnut Fudge

Prep Time: 10 mins

Cook Time: 10 mins

Total Time: 20 mins

Servings: 16 pieces

Ingredients:

- 2 cups of white chocolate chips
- 1 14-oz can sweetened condensed milk
- 1/3 cup of pure maple syrup
- 1/2 cup of chop-up walnuts
- 1 tsp vanilla extract

Instructions:

1. Leave enough parchment paper hanging over the sides of an 8x8-inch square baking pan to get the baked goods out without damaging the pan.
2. Add white chocolate chips and sweetened condensed milk to a medium saucepan and stir up to smooth. Stirring constantly, melt the chocolate in a saucepan over low heat up to it is completely smooth.
3. Combine the chop-up walnuts, pure maple syrup, and vanilla essence in a combining bowl.
4. Spread the Mixture evenly in the pan after pouring the Mixture in.
5. Fudge Must be chilled in the fridge for at least two hrs, or up to firm.
6. When the fudge has set, take it out of the pan by the parchment paper overhangs. Serve by slicing into squares.

Nutrition (per serving):
Cals: 216, Fat: 9g

Carbs: 29g

Protein: 3g

4.Mocha Almond Fudge

Prep Time: 10 mins

Cook Time: 10 mins

Total Time: 20 mins

Servings: 16 pieces

Ingredients:

- 2 cups of semi-sweet chocolate chips
- 1 14-oz can sweetened condensed milk
- 2 tbsp instant coffee granules
- 1/2 cup of chop-up almonds
- 1 tsp vanilla extract

Instructions:

1. Leave enough parchment paper hanging over the sides of an 8x8-inch square baking pan to get the baked goods out without damaging the pan.
2. Combine the semisweet chocolate chips and sweetened condensed milk in a medium saucepan. Stirring constantly, melt the chocolate in a saucepan over low heat up to it is completely smooth.
3. Blend in the ground coffee, almonds, and vanilla essence with a stir.
4. Spread the Mixture evenly in the pan after pouring the Mixture in.
5. Fudge Must be chilled in the fridge for at least two hrs, or up to firm.
6. When the fudge has set, take it out of the pan by the parchment paper overhangs. Serve by slicing into squares.

Nutrition (per serving):
Cals: 206, Fat: 11g

Carbs: 25g

Protein: 4g

5.Pecan Pie Fudge

Prep Time: 15 mins

Cook Time: 10 mins

Total Time: 25 mins

Servings: 16 pieces

Ingredients:

- 2 cups of chop-up pecans
- 1 cup of unsalted butter
- 1 cup of granulated sugar
- 1 cup of light brown sugar
- 2/3 cup of evaporated milk

- 1 tsp vanilla extract
- 2 cups of white chocolate chips
- 1 jar (7 ozs) marshmlet creme

Instructions:

1. Put parchment paper in an 8x8-inch baking dish and leave an overhang for lifting.
2. Melt the butter with the sugars and the brown sugar and the evaporated milk in a saucepan over medium heat. Achieve a rolling boil while stirring continuously. Prepare in 5 mins.
3. Once the white chocolate chips have dilute, turn off the heat and whisk them in. Combine in vanilla extract and marshmlet creme.
4. Add the chop-up pecans and combine gently.
5. When the Mixture has cooled to normal temperature, pour it into the baking dish.
6. Let at least 2 hrs in the fridge to set.
7. Slice the fudge into squares after removing it from the dish using the parchment paper.

Nutrition (per piece):
Cals: 287, Fat: 15g

Carbs: 36g

Protein: 2g

6.Eggnog Fudge

Prep Time: 10 mins

Cook Time: 10 mins

Total Time: 20 mins

Servings: 20 pieces

Ingredients:

- 2 1/2 cups of white chocolate chips
- 1/2 cup of unsalted butter
- 1 cup of granulated sugar
- 1/2 cup of eggnog
- 1/4 tsp ground nutmeg
- 1 tsp vanilla extract
- 1/2 cup of marshmlet creme

Instructions:

1. Put parchment paper in an 8x8-inch baking dish and leave an overhang for lifting.
2. Over medium heat, combine the butter, sugar, eggnog, and nutmeg in a saucepan. Achieve a rolling boil while stirring continuously. Prepare in 5 mins.
3. Once the white chocolate chips have dilute, turn off the heat and whisk them in. Combine in vanilla extract and marshmlet creme.
4. When the Mixture has cooled to normal temperature, pour it into the baking dish.
5. Let at least 2 hrs in the fridge to set.
6. Slice the fudge into squares after removing it from the dish using the parchment paper.

Nutrition (per piece):
Cals: 207, Fat: 11g

Carbs: 26g, Protein: 1g

7.Candy Cane Fudge

Prep Time: 15 mins

Cook Time: 10 mins

Total Time: 25 mins

Servings: 16 pieces

Ingredients:

- 2 cups of white chocolate chips
- 1/4 cup of unsalted butter
- 1 cup of granulated sugar
- 1/2 cup of heavy cream
- 1/4 tsp peppermint extract
- 1/2 cup of crushed candy canes

Instructions:

1. Put parchment paper in an 8x8-inch baking dish and leave an overhang for lifting.
2. Butter, sugar, heavy cream, and peppermint essence can be combined in a saucepan and heated over medium heat. Achieve a rolling boil while stirring continuously. Prepare in 5 mins.
3. Once the white chocolate chips have dilute, turn off the heat and whisk them in.
4. Combine in some crushed candy canes gently.
5. When the Mixture has cooled to normal temperature, pour it into the baking dish.
6. Let at least 2 hrs in the fridge to set.
7. Slice the fudge into squares after removing it from the dish using the parchment paper.

Nutrition (per piece):
Cals: 238, Fat: 11g

Carbs: 33g

Protein: 1g

8.Oreo Fudge

Prep Time: 15 mins

Cook Time: 10 mins

Total Time: 25 mins

Servings: 16 pieces

Ingredients:

- 3 cups of semisweet chocolate chips
- 1 can (14 ozs) sweetened condensed milk
- 1/4 cup of unsalted butter
- 2 tsp vanilla extract
- 15 Oreo cookies, crushed

Instructions:

1. Put parchment paper in an 8x8-inch baking dish and leave an overhang for lifting.

2. Sweetened condensed milk, chocolate chips, and butter are combined in a pot and heated over low heat. Blend together by stirring up to dilute.
3. Turn off the heat and combine in some vanilla extract and Oreo cookie crumbs.
4. When the Mixture has cooled to normal temperature, pour it into the baking dish.
5. Let at least 2 hrs in the fridge to set.
6. Slice the fudge into squares after removing it from the dish using the parchment paper.

Nutrition (per piece):
Cals: 285, Fat: 15g

Carbs: 35g

Protein: 3g

9.Classic Chocolate Fudge

Prep Time: 15 mins

Cook Time: 10 mins

Total Time: 25 mins

Servings: 16 pieces

Ingredients:

- 3 cups of semi-sweet chocolate chips
- 1 can (14 ozs) sweetened condensed milk
- 1/4 cup of unsalted butter
- 1 tsp pure vanilla extract
- 1/4 tsp salt

Instructions:

1. Melt the butter and sweetened condensed milk in a saucepan over low heat and stir in the chocolate chunks. Up to it has dilute and become smooth, stir constantly.
2. Take it off the fire and combine in some salt and vanilla extract.
3. Spread the batter evenly in an 8x8-inch pan that has been buttered.
4. Let it to cool for a few hrs at room temperature, or put it in the refrigerator to speed up the setting process.
5. When ready, slice the cake into 16 squares.

NUTRITION INFO (per serving):
Cals: 237, Fat: 12g

Carbs: 30g

Protein: 3g

10.Peppermint Bark Fudge

Prep Time: 15 mins

Cook Time: 10 mins

Total Time: 25 mins

Servings: 16 pieces

Ingredients:

- 3 cups of white chocolate chips
- 1 can (14 ozs) sweetened condensed milk
- 1/4 cup of unsalted butter
- 1 tsp peppermint extract
- 1/2 cup of crushed candy canes

Instructions:

1. Combine butter, sweetened condensed milk, and white chocolate chips in a saucepan and boil gently, stirring frequently. Keep stirring up to the Mixture is uniform.
2. Put the pan on a cool burner and add the peppermint extract.
3. Sprinkle the crushed candy canes on top and pour the Mixture into a buttered 8x8-inch pan.
4. Let it to cool to room temperature or place it in the fridge.
5. Serve by slicing into 16 pieces.

NUTRITION INFO (per serving):

Cals: 272, Fat: 13g

Carbs: 36g

Protein: 3g

11.White Chocolate Cranberry Fudge

Prep Time: 15 mins

Cook Time: 10 mins

Total Time: 25 mins

Servings: 16 pieces

Ingredients:

- 3 cups of white chocolate chips
- 1 can (14 ozs) sweetened condensed milk
- 1/4 cup of unsalted butter
- 1 tsp vanilla extract
- 1/2 cup of dried cranberries

Instructions:

1. Combine butter, sweetened condensed milk, and white chocolate chips in a saucepan and boil gently, stirring frequently. Keep stirring up to the Mixture is uniform.
2. Turn off the heat and combine in some dried cranberries and vanilla extract.
3. Put the batter into an 8x8 pan that has been buttered.
4. Let it to cool to room temperature or place it in the fridge.
5. Serve by slicing into 16 pieces.

NUTRITION INFO (per serving):

Cals: 267, Fat: 13g

Carbs: 34g

Protein: 3g

12.Gingerbread Fudge

Prep Time: 15 mins

Cook Time: 10 mins

Total Time: 25 mins

Servings: 16 pieces

Ingredients:

- 3 cups of white chocolate chips
- 1 can (14 ozs) sweetened condensed milk
- 1/4 cup of unsalted butter
- 1 tsp ground ginger
- 1 tsp ground cinnamon
- 1/4 tsp ground cloves
- 1/4 tsp ground nutmeg

Instructions:

1. Combine butter, sweetened condensed milk, and white chocolate chips in a saucepan and boil gently, stirring frequently. Keep stirring up to the Mixture is uniform.
2. Turn off the stove and add the ground spices (ginger, cinnamon, cloves, and nutmeg).
3. Put the batter into an 8x8 pan that has been buttered.
4. Let it to cool to room temperature or place it in the fridge.
5. Serve by slicing into 16 pieces.

NUTRITION INFO (per serving):

Cals: 263, Fat: 13g

Carbs: 35g

Protein: 3g

13.Toffee Crunch Fudge

Prep Time: 15 mins

Cook Time: 10 mins

Total Time: 2 hrs 25 mins (including cooling time) Servings: 16 pieces

Ingredients:

- 2 cups of semi-sweet chocolate chips
- 1 (14-oz) can sweetened condensed milk
- 1 tsp vanilla extract
- 1/2 cup of toffee bits
- 1/2 cup of chop-up nuts (non-compulsory)

Instructions:

1. Put some parchment paper or aluminum foil in an 8x8-inch baking sheet and leave an overhang for removing the baked goods.
2. Melt the sweetened condensed milk and chocolate chips together in a saucepan. The chocolate Must melt and the Mixture Must be smooth, so stir it up!

3. Turn off the heat and combine in the toffee pieces, vanilla essence, and chop-up nuts (if using).
4. Spread the fudge evenly in the prepared pan, then pour in the Mixture.
5. Let it to cool for at least two hrs, preferably longer.
6. When the fudge has cooled and set, take out it from the pan by lifting it with the overhanging paper or foil. Make 16 servings out of it.

14.Peppermint Mocha Fudge

Prep Time: 15 mins

Cook Time: 10 mins

Total Time: 2 hrs 25 mins (including cooling time) Servings: 16 pieces

Ingredients:
- 2 cups of semi-sweet chocolate chips
- 1 (14-oz) can sweetened condensed milk
- 1 tsp instant coffee granules
- 1/2 tsp peppermint extract
- 1/4 cup of crushed peppermint candies

Instructions:
1. To make, melt chocolate as directed for Toffee Crunch Fudge, then add instant coffee granules and peppermint extract.
2. Sprinkle the crushed peppermint candies on top of the fudge just before it sets.

15.Cinnamon Roll Fudge

Prep Time: 15 mins

Cook Time: 10 mins

Total Time: 2 hrs 25 mins (including cooling time) Servings: 16 pieces

Ingredients:
- 2 cups of white chocolate chips
- 1 (14-oz) can sweetened condensed milk
- 1 tsp ground cinnamon
- 1/2 tsp vanilla extract
- 1/4 cup of cream cheese frosting (store-bought or homemade)

Instructions:
1. White chocolate chips, ground cinnamon, and vanilla essence Must be dilute together in the same manner as in the recipe for Toffee Crunch Fudge.
2. While the fudge is still hot, top it with the cream cheese icing.

16.Cherry Almond Fudge

Prep Time: 15 mins

Cook Time: 10 mins

Total Time: 2 hrs 25 mins (including cooling time) Servings: 16 pieces

Ingredients:
- 2 cups of white chocolate chips
- 1 (14-oz) can sweetened condensed milk
- 1/2 tsp almond extract
- 1/2 cup of dried cherries, chop-up
- 1/2 cup of split almonds

Instructions:
1. Use white chocolate chips and add almond extract after the chocolate has dilute, then proceed as directed for Toffee Crunch Fudge.
2. Pour the Mixture into the prepared pan and stir in the split almonds and chop-up dried cherries.

17.Pumpkin Spice Fudge

Prep Time: 15 mins

Cook Time: 10 mins

Total Time: 25 mins

Servings: 24 pieces

Ingredients:
- 2 cups of white chocolate chips
- 1 cup of sweetened condensed milk
- 1/2 cup of canned pumpkin puree
- 1 tsp pumpkin pie spice
- 1 tsp vanilla extract
- 1/2 cup of chop-up pecans (non-compulsory)

Instructions:
1. For easier cleanup, use parchment paper to line an 8x8-inch square baking pan.
2. White chocolate chips and sweetened condensed milk Must be combined in a microwave-safe bowl. Stirring constantly, heat the Mixture in 30-second increments up to it is homogenous.
3. Blend the pumpkin puree with the pumpkin pie spice and vanilla extract.
4. Add the chop-up pecans if using.
5. Pour the batter into the dish and level it off.
6. Set in the fridge for at least 2 hrs.
7. Once the fudge has set, use the overhanging parchment paper to pull it off the pan.

Nutrition (per serving):
Cals: 138, Fat: 6g

Carbs: 19g

Protein: 2g

18. Butterscotch Pecan Fudge

Prep Time: 15 mins

Cook Time: 10 mins

Total Time: 25 mins

Servings: 24 pieces

Ingredients:
- 2 cups of butterscotch chips
- 1 cup of sweetened condensed milk
- 1/2 cup of chop-up pecans
- 1 tsp vanilla extract

Instructions:
1. For easier cleanup, use parchment paper to line an 8x8-inch square baking pan.
2. Put the butterscotch chips and sweetened condensed milk in a microwave-safe bowl and combine well. Stirring constantly, heat the Mixture in 30-second increments up to it is homogenous.
3. Blend in the chop-up nuts and vanilla extract using a spoon.
4. Pour the batter into the dish and level it off.
5. Set in the fridge for at least 2 hrs.
6. Once the fudge has set, use the overhanging parchment paper to pull it off the pan.

Nutrition (per serving):

Cals: 133, Fat: 7g

Carbs: 17g

Protein: 2g

19. Caramel Apple Fudge:

Prep Time: 15 mins

Cook Time: 10 mins

Total Time: 25 mins

Servings: About 16 pieces

Ingredients:
- 2 cups of white chocolate chips
- 1 can (14 ozs) sweetened condensed milk
- 1/2 cup of caramel sauce
- 1 cup of dried apple pieces
- 1/2 tsp apple pie spice

Instructions:
1. Prepare a parchment paper-lined 8x8-inch (20x20 cm) baking pan.
2. Stir continually while you melt white chocolate chips and sweetened condensed milk in a skillet over low heat.

3. Combine in the dried apples, caramel sauce, and apple pie spice.
4. After the pan has been prepped, pour the Mixture in and chill for at least 2 hrs to set.
5. Enjoy by slicing into squares.

20. Peanut Butter Cup of Fudge:

Prep Time: 15 mins

Cook Time: 10 mins

Total Time: 25 mins

Servings: About 16 pieces

Ingredients:
- 2 cups of semisweet chocolate chips
- 1 can (14 ozs) sweetened condensed milk
- 1 cup of peanut butter
- 1 cup of peanut butter cups of, chop-up

Instructions:
1. Prepare a parchment paper-lined 8x8-inch (20x20 cm) baking pan.
2. Stirring constantly, melt the chocolate chips and sweetened condensed milk in a saucepan over low heat.
3. Combine the peanut butter and the peanut butter cup of pieces in a combining bowl.
4. After the pan has been prepped, pour the Mixture in and chill for at least 2 hrs to set.
5. Enjoy by slicing into squares.

21. Chocolate Chip Cookie Dough Fudge:

Prep Time: 20 mins

Cook Time: 5 mins

Total Time: 25 mins

Servings: About 16 pieces

Ingredients:
- 2 cups of semisweet chocolate chips
- 1 can (14 ozs) sweetened condensed milk
- 1/2 cup of butter, melted
- 1 cup of brown sugar
- 1 cup of all-purpose flour
- 1/2 cup of mini chocolate chips
- 1 tsp vanilla extract

Instructions:
1. Prepare a parchment paper-lined 8x8-inch (20x20 cm) baking pan.
2. Stirring constantly, melt the chocolate chips and sweetened condensed milk in a saucepan over low heat.
3. Melted butter and brown sugar Must be beaten together in a separate basin up to smooth and creamy. Miniature chocolate chips, flour, and vanilla essence Must be stirred together.

4. Blend the cookie dough and chocolate together.
5. After the pan has been prepped, pour the Mixture in and chill for at least 2 hrs to set.
6. Enjoy by slicing into squares.

22. White Chocolate Peppermint Fudge:

Prep Time: 15 mins

Cook Time: 10 mins

Total Time: 25 mins

Servings: About 16 pieces

Ingredients:
- 2 cups of white chocolate chips
- 1 can (14 ozs) sweetened condensed milk
- 1/2 tsp peppermint extract
- 1/2 cup of crushed peppermint candies

Instructions:
1. Prepare a parchment paper-lined 8x8-inch (20x20 cm) baking pan.
2. Stir continually while you melt white chocolate chips and sweetened condensed milk in a skillet over low heat.
3. Combine in some crushed peppermint candies and peppermint essence.
4. After the pan has been prepped, pour the Mixture in and chill for at least 2 hrs to set.
5. Enjoy by slicing into squares.

23. Marshmlet Swirl Fudge

Prep Time: 15 mins

Cook Time: 10 mins

Total Time: 25 mins

Servings: 16 pieces

Ingredients:
- 3 cups of semi-sweet chocolate chips
- 1 can (14 oz) sweetened condensed milk
- 1/4 cup of unsalted butter
- 1 tsp vanilla extract
- 2 cups of mini marshmlets

Instructions:
1. Melt the butter, sweetened condensed milk, and chocolate chips in a saucepan over low heat. Combine thoroughly.
2. Take it off the stove and combine in some vanilla extract.
3. Mini marshmlets Must be folded in after the Mixture has cooled for a few mins.
4. Spread the fudge batter in a buttered 8x8-inch pan.
5. Put in the fridge and chill for at least 2 hrs, preferably longer.

6. Serve by slicing into squares.

24. Coconut Macaroon Fudge

Prep Time: 10 mins

Cook Time: 10 mins

Total Time: 20 mins

Servings: 16 pieces

Ingredients:
- 3 cups of white chocolate chips
- 1 can (14 oz) sweetened condensed milk
- 1 tsp vanilla extract
- 1 1/2 cups of shredded coconut

Instructions:
1. White chocolate chips and sweetened condensed milk Must be dilute together in a saucepan over low heat. Combine thoroughly.
2. Turn off the heat and combine in some shredded coconut and vanilla extract.
3. Spread the fudge batter in a buttered 8x8-inch pan.
4. Put in the fridge and chill for at least 2 hrs, preferably longer.
5. Serve by slicing into squares.

24. Salted Pretzel Fudge

Prep Time: 15 mins

Cook Time: 10 mins

Total Time: 25 mins

Servings: 16 pieces

Ingredients:
- 3 cups of semi-sweet chocolate chips
- 1 can (14 oz) sweetened condensed milk
- 1/4 cup of unsalted butter
- 1 tsp vanilla extract
- 1 cup of crushed pretzels
- Sea salt for sprinkling

Instructions:
1. Melt the butter, sweetened condensed milk, and chocolate chips in a saucepan over low heat. Combine thoroughly.
2. Take off the stove and combine in some vanilla extract and crushed pretzels.
3. Spread the fudge batter in a buttered 8x8-inch pan.
4. Add a pinch of salt from the sea.
5. Put in the fridge and chill for at least 2 hrs, preferably longer.
6. Serve by slicing into squares.

25. Cranberry Orange Fudge

Prep Time: 15 mins

Cook Time: 10 mins

Total Time: 25 mins

Servings: 16 pieces

Ingredients:

- 3 cups of white chocolate chips
- 1 can (14 oz) sweetened condensed milk
- Zest of 1 orange
- 1/2 cup of dried cranberries

Instructions:

1. Melt the white chocolate chips and sweetened condensed milk in a saucepan over low heat. Up to smooth, stir.
2. Take off the heat and combine in the dried cranberries and orange zest.
3. Fill an 8x8-inch baking pan with the fudge Mixture once it has been buttered.
4. Chill for about two hrs in the refrigerator, or up to set.
5. Serve after Cutting into squares.

26. Rocky Road Fudge

Prep Time: 10 mins

Cook Time: 5 mins

Total Time: 2 hrs

Servings: 16 pieces

Ingredients:

- 3 cups of semi-sweet chocolate chips
- 1 can (14 ozs) sweetened condensed milk
- 1 tsp vanilla extract
- 1 1/2 cups of miniature marshmlets
- 1/2 cup of chop-up nuts (e.g., walnuts or almonds)

Instructions:

1. Prepare a parchment paper-lined 8x8-inch baking tray.
2. Melt the sweetened condensed milk and chocolate chips together in a microwave-safe bowl.
3. Stirring after every 30 seconds in the microwave will result in a smooth, dilute Mixture.
4. Add the vanilla, marshmlets, and chop-up nuts and combine well.
5. Then, evenly distribute the Mixture in the baking dish.
6. Fudge Must be chilled in the fridge for at least two hrs, or up to firm.
7. Once it has hardened, slice it into squares and serve.

Nutrition (per serving):

Cals: 230, Fat: 11g

Carbs: 32g, Protein: 3g

27. Snickerdoodle Fudge

Prep Time: 15 mins

Cook Time: 5 mins

Total Time: 2 hrs

Servings: 16 pieces

Ingredients:

- 2 cups of white chocolate chips
- 1 can (14 ozs) sweetened condensed milk
- 1 tsp vanilla extract
- 1 tsp ground cinnamon
- 1/4 cup of granulated sugar
- 1 tbsp ground cinnamon (for rolling)

Instructions:

1. Prepare a parchment paper-lined 8x8-inch baking tray.
2. White chocolate chips and sweetened condensed milk Must be combined in a microwave-safe bowl.
3. Stirring after every 30 seconds in the microwave will result in a smooth, dilute Mixture.
4. Combine in 1 tsp of ground cinnamon and the vanilla extract.
5. Put the contents of the bowl into the baking dish.
6. Combine the granulated sugar and ground cinnamon in a mini bowl.
7. The fudge would benefit with a dusting of the cinnamon sugar.
8. Fudge Must be chilled in the fridge for at least two hrs, or up to firm.
9. Enjoy by slicing into squares.

Nutrition (per serving):

Cals: 220, Fat: 10g

Carbs: 30g

Protein: 3g

28. Chocolate Orange Fudge

Prep Time: 15 mins

Cook Time: 5 mins

Total Time: 2 hrs

Servings: 16 pieces

Ingredients:

- 2 cups of semi-sweet chocolate chips
- 1 can (14 ozs) sweetened condensed milk
- 1 tsp orange extract or orange zest
- 1/4 cup of candied orange peel (non-compulsory)

Instructions:

1. Prepare a parchment paper-lined 8x8-inch baking tray.
2. Melt the sweetened condensed milk and

chocolate chips together in a microwave-safe bowl.

3. Stirring after every 30 seconds in the microwave will result in a smooth, dilute Mixture.
4. Toss in the candied orange peel and orange extract/zest, if using.
5. Then, evenly distribute the Mixture in the baking dish.
6. Fudge Must be chilled in the fridge for at least two hrs, or up to firm.
7. Enjoy by slicing into squares.

Nutrition (per serving):

Cals: 180, Fat: 8g

Carbs: 26g

Protein: 3g

29. Nutella Swirl Fudge

Prep Time: 15 mins

Cook Time: 5 mins

Total Time: 2 hrs

Servings: 16 pieces

Ingredients:

- 2 cups of semi-sweet chocolate chips
- 1 can (14 ozs) sweetened condensed milk
- 1/2 cup of Nutella (hazelnut spread)
- 1 tsp vanilla extract

Instructions:

1. Prepare a parchment paper-lined 8x8-inch baking tray.
2. Melt the sweetened condensed milk and chocolate chips together in a microwave-safe bowl.
3. Stirring after every 30 seconds in the microwave will result in a smooth, dilute Mixture.
4. Add the vanilla extract and combine it up.
5. Put the contents of the bowl into the baking dish.
6. Spoon some Nutella onto the fudge, then use a butter knife to make swirls in it.
7. Fudge Must be chilled in the fridge for at least two hrs, or up to firm.
8. Enjoy by slicing into squares.

Nutrition (per serving):

Cals: 210, Fat: 11g

Carbs: 28g

Protein: 3g

30. Cookies and Cream Fudge

Prep Time: 15 mins

Cook Time: 10 mins

Total Time: 25 mins

Servings: About 36 pieces

Ingredients:

- 3 cups of white chocolate chips
- 1 can (14 ozs) sweetened condensed milk
- 2 tsp pure vanilla extract
- 15 chocolate sandwich cookies, crushed

Instructions:

1. Leave an overhang on both edges of a square 8x8-inch (20x20 centimeter) baking pan for easy removal of the baked goods.
2. Stirring constantly, melt the white chocolate chips and sweetened condensed milk in a medium saucepan over low heat.
3. Take it off the stove and combine in some vanilla extract.
4. Combine the chocolate sandwich cookies by gently folding them in.
5. Then, evenly distribute the Mixture in the baking dish.
6. Set in the fridge for at least two hrs, preferably three.
7. When the fudge has set, take out it from the pan by lifting up on the overhanging parchment paper. Make tiny squares using it.
8. Put the Cookies and Cream Fudge in a sealed container and place it in the fridge.

Nutrition (per serving, based on 36 servings):

Cals: Approximately 130

Fat: Approximately 6g

Carbs: Approximately 18g

Protein: Approximately 2g

31. White Chocolate Raspberry Fudge

Prep Time: 10 mins

Cook Time: 10 mins

Total Time: 20 mins

Servings: About 36 pieces

Ingredients:

- 3 cups of white chocolate chips
- 1 can (14 ozs) sweetened condensed milk
- 1 tsp pure vanilla extract
- 1 cup of freeze-dried raspberries

Instructions:

1. Leave an overhang on both edges of a square 8x8-inch (20x20 centimeter) baking pan for easy removal of the baked goods.
2. Stirring constantly, melt the white chocolate chips and sweetened condensed milk in a medium saucepan over low heat.
3. Take it off the stove and combine in some vanilla extract.
4. Add the freeze-dried raspberries and combine gently.

5. Then, evenly distribute the Mixture in the baking dish.
6. Set in the fridge for at least two hrs, preferably three.
7. When the fudge has set, take out it from the pan by lifting up on the overhanging parchment paper. Make tiny squares using it.
8. White Chocolate Raspberry Fudge Must be kept in the fridge in an airtight container.

Nutrition (per serving, based on 36 servings):
Cals: Approximately 120
Fat: Approximately 5g
Carbs: Approximately 18g
Protein: Approximately 2g

32.Peanut Butter and Jelly Fudge

Prep Time: 10 mins
Cook Time: 5 mins
Total Time: 3 hrs 15 mins (including chilling)
Servings: 16 pieces

Ingredients:
- 2 cups of creamy peanut butter
- 1/2 cup of unsalted butter
- 4 cups of powdered sugar
- 1 tsp vanilla extract
- 1/2 cup of raspberry jam (or your preferred flavor)
- Pinch of salt

Instructions:
1. Prepare a square 8x8-inch (20x20 cm) baking pan with parchment paper, leting a little extra paper to hang over two opposite sides for lifting.
2. Combine the peanut butter and butter in a microwave-safe bowl. Stirring constantly, heat in 30-second increments up to smooth.
3. Combine in the confectioners' sugar, vanilla essence, and a little salt up to everything is evenly distributed.
4. Two-thirds of the peanut butter Mixture Must be pressed firmly into the bottom of the prepared pan.
5. Spread the jam over the peanut butter after warming it for 20 to 30 seconds in the microwave to soften it.
6. Spoon the remaining peanut butter Mixture over the jam and use a knife or skewer to stir the two together.
7. Cover and chill for at least 3 hrs, or up to firm.
8. Using the overhanging parchment paper, carefully take out the fudge from the pan and slice it into pieces.
9. Put away in a sealed container.

Nutrition (per serving, approximate):
Cals: 290, Fat: 18g
Carbs: 29g
Protein: 6g

33.S'mores Fudge

Prep Time: 10 mins
Cook Time: 5 mins
Total Time: 2 hrs 15 mins (including chilling)
Servings: 16 pieces

Ingredients:
- 2 cups of milk chocolate chips
- 1 cup of semi-sweet chocolate chips
- One 14-ounce can of sweetened condensed milk
- 1 tsp pure vanilla extract
- 1 cup of mini marshmlets
- 1 cup of crushed graham crackers

Instructions:
1. Prepare a square 8x8-inch (20x20 cm) baking pan with parchment paper, leting a little extra paper to hang over two opposite sides for lifting.
2. Melt the sweetened condensed milk and chocolate chips together in a microwave-safe bowl. Stirring constantly, heat in 30-second increments up to smooth.
3. Add the vanilla extract and combine it up.
4. Combine in the marshmlets and graham cracker crumbs very gently.
5. Coat the bottom and sides of the pan with the Mixture.
6. Set in the fridge for at least 2 hrs.
7. Using the overhanging parchment paper, carefully take out the fudge from the pan and slice it into pieces.
8. Put away in a sealed container.

Nutrition (per serving, approximate):
Cals: 275, Fat: 11g
Carbs: 42g
Protein: 4g

34.White Chocolate Cinnamon Fudge

Prep Time: 10 mins
Cook Time: 5 mins
Total Time: 3 hrs 15 mins (including chilling)
Servings: 16 pieces

Ingredients:
- 2 cups of white chocolate chips

- One 14-ounce can of sweetened condensed milk
- 1 tsp ground cinnamon
- 1 tsp vanilla extract
- Pinch of salt

Instructions:

1. Prepare a square 8x8-inch (20x20 cm) baking pan with parchment paper, leting a little extra paper to hang over two opposite sides for lifting.
2. White chocolate chips and sweetened condensed milk Must be combined in a microwave-safe bowl. Stirring constantly, heat in 30-second increments up to smooth.
3. Add the ground cinnamon, vanilla extract, and a bit of salt, and stir to combine.
4. Coat the bottom and sides of the pan with the Mixture.
5. Cover and chill for at least 3 hrs, or up to firm.
6. Using the overhanging parchment paper, carefully take out the fudge from the pan and slice it into pieces.
7. Put away in a sealed container.

Nutrition (per serving, approximate):

Cals: 260, Fat: 11g

Carbs: 38g

Protein: 3g

35.Hazelnut Chocolate Fudge

Prep Time: 10 mins

Cook Time: 5 mins

Total Time: 3 hrs 15 mins (including chilling)

Servings: 16 pieces

Ingredients:

- 2 cups of semi-sweet chocolate chips
- 1 can (14 ozs) sweetened condensed milk
- 1/2 cup of hazelnut spread (e.g., Nutella)
- 1 tsp vanilla extract
- 1/2 cup of chop-up roasted hazelnuts
- Pinch of salt

Instructions:

1. Prepare a square 8x8-inch (20x20 cm) baking pan with parchment paper, leting a little extra paper to hang over two opposite sides for lifting.
2. Melt the sweetened condensed milk and chocolate chips together in a microwave-safe bowl. Stirring constantly, heat in 30-second increments up to smooth.
3. Combine in some chop-up hazelnuts, vanilla extract, and salt into the hazelnut spread.
4. Coat the bottom and sides of the pan with the Mixture.
5. Cover and chill for at least 3 hrs, or up to firm.

6. Using the overhanging parchment paper, carefully take out the fudge from the pan and slice it into pieces.
7. Put away in a sealed container.

Nutrition (per serving, approximate):

Cals: 280, Fat: 13g

Carbs: 37g

Protein: 4g

36.Raspberry Cheesecake Fudge

Prep Time: 15 mins

Cook Time: 5 mins

Total Time: 20 mins

Servings: 16 pieces

Ingredients:

- 2 cups of white chocolate chips
- 1 can (14 oz) sweetened condensed milk
- 1/2 cup of raspberry jam
- 1 cup of graham cracker crumbs
- 1/2 cup of fresh raspberries (for garnish)

Instructions:

1. Prepare a parchment paper-lined 8x8-inch baking tray.
2. White chocolate chips and sweetened condensed milk Must be dilute together in a microwave-safe bowl at 30-second intervals, stirred between every, up to smooth.
3. Combine the graham cracker crumbs and raspberry jam by stirring them together.
4. Spread the Mixture evenly in the pan after pouring the Mixture in.
5. Sprinkle some raw raspberries on top.
6. Fudge Must be chilled in the fridge for at least two hrs, or up to firm.
7. Enjoy by slicing into squares.

Nutrition (per serving):

Cals: 250, Fat: 11g

Carbs: 35g

Protein: 4g

37.Hot Cocoa Fudge

Prep Time: 10 mins

Cook Time: 5 mins

Total Time: 15 mins

Servings: 24 pieces

Ingredients:

- 3 cups of semisweet chocolate chips
- 1 can (14 oz) sweetened condensed milk
- 1/4 cup of unsweetened cocoa powder
- 1/4 cup of mini marshmlets (for topping)

Instructions:

1. Prepare a parchment paper-lined 9x9-inch baking pan.
2. The chocolate chips and sweetened condensed milk Must be dilute in the microwave in 30-second increments, stirred between every, up to smooth.
3. Add the chocolate powder and combine thoroughly.
4. Spread the Mixture evenly in the pan after pouring the Mixture in.
5. Mini marshmlets, please.
6. Fudge Must be chilled in the fridge for at least two hrs, or up to firm.
7. Enjoy by slicing into squares.

Nutrition (per serving):

Cals: 180, Fat: 9g

Carbs: 25g

Protein: 3g

38.Andes Mint Fudge

Prep Time: 10 mins

Cook Time: 5 mins

Total Time: 15 mins

Servings: 24 pieces

Ingredients:

- 2 cups of semisweet chocolate chips
- 1 can (14 oz) sweetened condensed milk
- 1 tsp peppermint extract
- 1 cup of Andes mint chocolate pieces (chop-up)

Instructions:

1. Prepare a parchment paper-lined 9x9-inch baking pan.
2. The chocolate chips and sweetened condensed milk Must be dilute in the microwave in 30-second increments, stirred between every, up to smooth.
3. Peppermint extract and Andean mint Must be combined in at this point.
4. Spread the Mixture evenly in the pan after pouring the Mixture in.
5. Fudge Must be chilled in the fridge for at least two hrs, or up to firm.
6. Enjoy by slicing into squares.

Nutrition (per serving):

Cals: 180, Fat: 9g

Carbs: 24g

Protein: 2g

39.Tiramisu Fudge

Prep Time: 15 mins

Cook Time: 5 mins

Total Time: 20 mins

Servings: 16 pieces

Ingredients:

- 2 cups of white chocolate chips
- 1 can (14 oz) sweetened condensed milk
- 1 tsp instant coffee granules
- 1/4 cup of ladyfingers (crushed)
- 1 tbsp cocoa powder (for dusting)

Instructions:

1. Prepare a parchment paper-lined 8x8-inch baking tray.
2. White chocolate chips and sweetened condensed milk Must be dilute together in a microwave-safe bowl at 30-second intervals, stirred between every, up to smooth.
3. Combine in the crushed ladyfingers and instant coffee granules.
4. Spread the Mixture evenly in the pan after pouring the Mixture in.
5. Sprinkle some chocolate powder on top.
6. Fudge Must be chilled in the fridge for at least two hrs, or up to firm.
7. Enjoy by slicing into squares.

Nutrition (per serving):

Cals: 230, Fat: 11g

Carbs: 31g

Protein: 4g

40.Key Lime Pie Fudge

Prep Time: 15 mins

Cook Time: 10 mins

Total Time: 2 hrs and 25 mins

Servings: 24 squares

Ingredients:

- 2 cups of white chocolate chips
- 1 (14 ozs) can sweetened condensed milk
- 1/4 cup of unsalted butter
- 1 tbsp lime zest
- 1/3 cup of key lime juice
- 1/2 cup of graham cracker crumbs

Instructions:

1. Prepare a square 8x8-inch baking pan by lining it with parchment paper and leting it to dangle over two opposite sides.
2. Melt the butter and sweetened condensed milk in a saucepan and add the white chocolate chips. Stirring constantly, melt over low heat up to smooth.
3. Add key lime juice and lime zest and stir. Maintain a healthy blend.

4. Prepare a pan by adding half of the fudge Mixture.
5. Divide the graham cracker crumbs in half and spread half of them evenly over the fudge.
6. The remaining fudge Mixture can be poured on top and spread out evenly.
7. The remaining graham cracker crumbs Must be sprinkled on top.
8. Refrigerate for at least 2 hrs, or up to desired consistency is reveryed.
9. Fudge may be take outd from the pan by using the overhanging parchment paper and then slice into squares.

Nutrition (per serving):
Cals: 189, Fat: 10g

Carbs: 22g

Protein: 2g

41. Lemon Blueberry Fudge

Prep Time: 10 mins

Cook Time: 5 mins

Total Time: 2 hrs and 15 mins

Servings: 24 squares

Ingredients:
- 2 cups of white chocolate chips
- 1 (14 ozs) can sweetened condensed milk
- 1/4 cup of unsalted butter
- 1 tbsp lemon zest
- 1/2 cup of dried blueberries

Instructions:
1. Prepare a square 8x8-inch baking pan by lining it with parchment paper and leting it to dangle over two opposite sides.
2. Melt the butter and sweetened condensed milk in a saucepan and add the white chocolate chips. Stirring constantly, melt over low heat up to smooth.
3. Blend in some dried blueberries and lemon zest. Maintain a healthy blend.
4. When the pan is ready, pour in the fudge Mixture and spread it out evenly.
5. Refrigerate for at least 2 hrs, or up to desired consistency is reveryed.
6. Fudge may be take outd from the pan by using the overhanging parchment paper and then slice into squares.

Nutrition (per serving):
Cals: 182, Fat: 9g

Carbs: 23g

Protein: 2g

42. Cranberry Pistachio Fudge

Prep Time: 15 mins

Cook Time: 10 mins

Total Time: 2 hrs and 25 mins

Servings: 24 squares

Ingredients:
- 2 cups of white chocolate chips
- 1 (14 ozs) can sweetened condensed milk
- 1/4 cup of unsalted butter
- 1/2 cup of dried cranberries
- 1/2 cup of chop-up pistachios

Instructions:
1. Prepare a square 8x8-inch baking pan by lining it with parchment paper and leting it to dangle over two opposite sides.
2. Melt the butter and sweetened condensed milk in a saucepan and add the white chocolate chips. Stirring constantly, melt over low heat up to smooth.
3. Blend with some pistachios and dried berries. Maintain a healthy blend.
4. When the pan is ready, pour in the fudge Mixture and spread it out evenly.
5. Refrigerate for at least 2 hrs, or up to desired consistency is reveryed.
6. Fudge may be take outd from the pan by using the overhanging parchment paper and then slice into squares.

Nutrition (per serving):
Cals: 197, Fat: 10g

Carbs: 24g

Protein: 2g

43. Mint Chocolate Swirl Fudge

Prep Time: 15 mins

Cook Time: 10 mins

Total Time: 2 hrs and 25 mins

Servings: 24 squares

Ingredients:
- 2 cups of semi-sweet chocolate chips
- 2 cups of white chocolate chips
- 1 (14 ozs) can sweetened condensed milk
- 1/4 cup of unsalted butter
- 1 tsp peppermint extract
- Green food coloring (non-compulsory)

Instructions:
1. Prepare a square 8x8-inch baking pan by lining it with parchment paper and leting it to dangle over two opposite sides.
2. Slightly sweet chocolate chips, sweetened condensed milk, and half the butter Must be

dilute in a skillet over low heat, then stirred up to smooth.

3. White chocolate chips, the remaining butter, and the peppermint extract Must be dilute together in a separate skillet. The non-compulsory addition of green food coloring.

4. Once the pan has been prepped, pour in the semisweet chocolate Mixture.

5. White chocolate with a minty flavor Must be poured on top, and the two layers Must be swirled together with a knife.

6. Refrigerate for at least 2 hrs, or up to desired consistency is reveryed.

7. Fudge may be take outd from the pan by using the overhanging parchment paper and then slice into squares.

Nutrition (per serving):

Cals: 218, Fat: 12g

Carbs: 26g

Protein: 2g

44.Caramel Popcorn Fudge:

Prep Time: 15 mins

Cook Time: 10 mins

Total Time: 25 mins

Servings: 12 pieces

Ingredients:

- 3 cups of white chocolate chips
- 1 can (14 ozs) of sweetened condensed milk
- 1/2 cup of of caramel sauce
- 2 cups of popped popcorn
- 1/2 cup of of chop-up caramel candies

Instructions:

1. Prepare a square 8x8-inch baking pan by lining it with parchment paper and leting an overhang on two opposite sides.

2. White chocolate chips and sweetened condensed milk Must be combined in a microwave-safe bowl. To achieve a smooth consistency, microwave in 30-second increments while stirring after every.

3. Add the caramel sauce and combine thoroughly.

4. Combine in the caramel candies and popcorn with care.

5. Spread the fudge evenly in the prepared pan, then pour in the Mixture.

6. Let it to cool for at least two hrs, preferably longer.

7. Once the fudge has set, you can use the overhanging parchment paper to take out it from the pan. Enjoy by slicing into squares.

NUTRITION INFO (per serving):

Cals: 320, Fat: 14g

Carbs: 46g, Protein: 5g

45.Mocha Peppermint Fudge:

Prep Time: 20 mins

Cook Time: 5 mins

Total Time: 25 mins

Servings: 16 pieces

Ingredients:

- 2 cups of semi-sweet chocolate chips
- 1 can (14 ozs) of sweetened condensed milk
- 2 tsp of instant coffee granules
- 1/2 tsp of peppermint extract
- 1/4 cup of of crushed peppermint candies

Instructions:

1. Prepare a square 8x8-inch baking pan by lining it with parchment paper and leting an overhang on two opposite sides.

2. Put the instant coffee granules in a microwave-safe bowl and add the sweetened condensed milk and semisweet chocolate chunks. To achieve a smooth consistency, microwave in 30-second increments while stirring after every.

3. Peppermint extract Must be combined in now.

4. Spread the fudge evenly in the prepared pan, then pour in the Mixture.

5. Peppermint candy crumbs can be sprinkled on top.

6. Let it to cool for at least two hrs, preferably longer.

7. Once the fudge has set, you can use the overhanging parchment paper to take out it from the pan. Enjoy by slicing into squares.

NUTRITION INFO (per serving):

Cals: 180, Fat: 7g

Carbs: 29g

Protein: 2g

46.Coconut Lime Fudge:

Prep Time: 15 mins

Cook Time: 5 mins

Total Time: 20 mins

Servings: 16 pieces

Ingredients:

- 2 cups of white chocolate chips
- 1 can (14 ozs) of sweetened condensed milk
- 1/2 cup of of shredded coconut
- Zest of 2 limes
- 2 tbsp of lime juice

Instructions:

1. Prepare a square 8x8-inch baking pan by lining it with parchment paper and leting an overhang on two opposite sides.
2. White chocolate chips and sweetened condensed milk Must be combined in a microwave-safe bowl. To achieve a smooth consistency, microwave in 30-second increments while stirring after every.
3. Combine the shredded coconut, lime juice, and lime zest in a bowl.
4. Spread the fudge evenly in the prepared pan, then pour in the Mixture.
5. Let it to cool for at least two hrs, preferably longer.
6. Once the fudge has set, you can use the overhanging parchment paper to take out it from the pan. Enjoy by slicing into squares.

NUTRITION INFO (per serving):

Cals: 200, Fat: 8g

Carbs: 29g

Protein: 3g

47.Red Hot Cinnamon Fudge:

Prep Time: 15 mins

Cook Time: 5 mins

Total Time: 20 mins

Servings: 16 pieces

Ingredients:

- 2 cups of white chocolate chips
- 1 can (14 ozs) of sweetened condensed milk
- 1/2 tsp of ground cinnamon
- 1/4 tsp of cayenne pepper (adjust as needed)
- Red food coloring (non-compulsory, for color)

Instructions:

1. Prepare a square 8x8-inch baking pan by lining it with parchment paper and leting an overhang on two opposite sides.
2. White chocolate chips and sweetened condensed milk Must be combined in a microwave-safe bowl. To achieve a smooth consistency, microwave in 30-second increments while stirring after every.
3. Combine with some ground cayenne pepper and cinnamon. If you want it redder, add more food coloring.
4. Spread the fudge evenly in the prepared pan, then pour in the Mixture.
5. Let it to cool for at least two hrs, preferably longer.

6. Once the fudge has set, you can use the overhanging parchment paper to take out it from the pan. Enjoy by slicing into squares.

NUTRITION INFO (per serving):

Cals: 180, Fat: 7g

Carbs: 28g, Protein: 3g

48.Chai Spice Fudge

Prep Time: 15 mins

Cook Time: 10 mins

Total Time: 25 mins

Servings: 16 pieces

Ingredients:

- 2 cups of white chocolate chips
- 1/4 cup of sweetened condensed milk
- 1 tsp chai spice combine (cinnamon, cardamom, ginger, cloves, and nutmeg)
- 1/2 cup of chop-up nuts (e.g., almonds, cashews)
- 1/4 cup of chop-up dried cranberries
- 1 tsp vanilla extract

Instructions:

1. Prepare a parchment paper-lined 8x8-inch (20x20 cm) baking pan.
2. White chocolate chips and sweetened condensed milk Must be dilute together in a microwave-safe bowl at 30-second intervals up to smooth.
3. Combine in some vanilla extract and chai spice blend.
4. Combine the nuts and cranberries by combining them in.
5. Spread the Mixture evenly in the pan after pouring the Mixture in.
6. Put in the fridge and chill for at least 2 hrs.
7. Divide into 16 equal pieces and relish.

NUTRITION INFO (per serving):

Cals: Approximately 200

Fat: 12g, Carbs: 20g

Protein: 3g

49.Pistachio Cranberry Fudge

Prep Time: 15 mins

Cook Time: 10 mins

Total Time: 25 mins

Servings: 16 pieces

Ingredients:

- 2 cups of white chocolate chips
- 1/4 cup of sweetened condensed milk
- 1/2 cup of shelled pistachios, chop-up
- 1/2 cup of dried cranberries
- 1 tsp vanilla extract

Instructions:

1. Prepare a parchment paper-lined 8x8-inch (20x20 cm) baking pan.
2. White chocolate chips and sweetened condensed milk Must be dilute together in a microwave-safe bowl at 30-second intervals up to smooth.
3. Add the vanilla extract and combine it up.
4. Combine the pistachios and cranberries by folding them in.
5. Spread the Mixture evenly in the pan after pouring the Mixture in.
6. Put in the fridge and chill for at least 2 hrs.
7. Divide into 16 equal pieces and relish.

NUTRITION INFO (per serving):

Cals: Approximately 220

Fat: 13g, Carbs: 25g

Protein: 4g

50.Sugar Cookie Fudge

Prep Time: 10 mins

Cook Time: 5 mins

Total Time: 15 mins

Servings: 16 pieces

Ingredients:

- 2 cups of white chocolate chips
- 1/4 cup of sweetened condensed milk
- 1/2 cup of crushed sugar cookies
- 1/4 cup of rainbow sprinkles
- 1 tsp vanilla extract

Instructions:

1. Prepare a parchment paper-lined 8x8-inch (20x20 cm) baking pan.
2. White chocolate chips and sweetened condensed milk Must be dilute together in a microwave-safe bowl at 30-second intervals up to smooth.
3. Add the vanilla extract and combine it up.
4. Combine the cookie crumbs and sprinkles.
5. Spread the Mixture evenly in the pan after pouring the Mixture in.
6. Put in the fridge and chill for at least 2 hrs.
7. Divide into 16 equal pieces and relish.

NUTRITION INFO (per serving):

Cals: Approximately 200

Fat: 10g, Carbs: 25g

Protein: 2g

51.Buttermint Fudge

Prep Time: 15 mins

Cook Time: 10 mins

Total Time: 25 mins

Servings: 16 pieces

Ingredients:

- 2 cups of white chocolate chips
- 1/4 cup of sweetened condensed milk
- 1/2 tsp peppermint extract
- 1/4 cup of butter mints (crushed)
- A few drops of green food coloring (non-compulsory)

Instructions:

1. Prepare a parchment paper-lined 8x8-inch (20x20 cm) baking pan.
2. White chocolate chips and sweetened condensed milk Must be dilute together in a microwave-safe bowl at 30-second intervals up to smooth.
3. Peppermint extract and green dye (if using) Must be combined in.
4. Combine in the butter mints that you crushed.
5. Spread the Mixture evenly in the pan after pouring the Mixture in.
6. Put in the fridge and chill for at least 2 hrs.
7. Divide into 16 equal pieces and relish.

NUTRITION INFO (per serving):

Cals: Approximately 180

Fat: 8g, Carbs: 25g

Protein: 2g

52.Chocolate Covered Strawberry Fudge

Prep Time: 15 mins

Cook Time: 10 mins

Total Time: 25 mins

Servings: 16 pieces

Ingredients:

- 2 cups of semi-sweet chocolate chips
- A 14-oz can of condensed milk that has been sweetened
- 1 cup of freeze-dried strawberries
- 1 tsp vanilla extract
- A pinch of salt

Instructions:

1. Prepare a parchment paper-lined 8-inch square baking dish.
2. Melt the sweetened condensed milk and chocolate chips together in a microwave-safe bowl. Stirring after every 30 second microwave interval will ensure a smooth and dilute Mixture.
3. Add a dash of salt and the vanilla extract and stir to combine.
4. The freeze-dried strawberries Must be folded in well.
5. Toss everything together and spread it out in the baking dish.
6. Put in the fridge and chill for a minimum of 2 hrs.

7. When ready, divide into 16 equal parts.

Nutrition (per serving):
Cals: 200, Fat: 9g

Carbs: 28g, Protein: 3g

53.Brownie Batter Fudge

Prep Time: 10 mins

Cook Time: 5 mins

Total Time: 15 mins

Servings: 24 pieces

Ingredients:
- 1 1/2 cups of semi-sweet chocolate chips
- A 14-oz can of condensed milk that has been sweetened
- 1/4 cup of unsweetened cocoa powder
- 1/4 cup of all-purpose flour
- 1/4 cup of mini chocolate chips
- 1 tsp vanilla extract
- A pinch of salt

Instructions:
1. Prepare a parchment paper-lined 8-inch square baking dish.
2. Combine the semisweet chocolate chips and sweetened condensed milk in a microwave-safe bowl. Melt in the microwave at 30-second intervals, stirring after every, up to smooth.
3. Combine the flour, cocoa powder, chocolate chips, vanilla essence, and salt in a bowl and stir.
4. Toss everything together and spread it out in the baking dish.
5. Put in the fridge and chill for a minimum of 2 hrs.
6. Break up into 24 servings.

Nutrition (per serving):
Cals: 150, Fat: 6g

Carbs: 23g

Protein: 3g

54.Maple Bacon Fudge

Prep Time: 15 mins

Cook Time: 5 mins

Total Time: 20 mins

Servings: 20 pieces

Ingredients:
- 2 cups of white chocolate chips
- One 14-ounce can of sweetened condensed milk
- 1/4 cup of pure maple syrup
- 1/2 cup of cooked and cut up bacon
- 1 tsp vanilla extract

Instructions:
1. Prepare a parchment paper-lined 8-inch square baking dish.
2. White chocolate chips and sweetened condensed milk Must be combined in a microwave-safe bowl. Melt in the microwave at 30-second intervals, stirring after every, up to smooth.
3. Combine in the shredded bacon, pure maple syrup, and vanilla extract.
4. Toss everything together and spread it out in the baking dish.
5. Put in the fridge and chill for a minimum of 2 hrs.
6. Prepare 20 servings.

Nutrition (per serving):
Cals: 180, Fat: 8g

Carbs: 24g

Protein: 4g

55.Almond Joyful Fudge

Prep Time: 15 mins

Cook Time: 10 mins

Total Time: 25 mins

Servings: 16 squares

Ingredients:
- 3 cups of semi-sweet chocolate chips
- A 14-oz can of condensed sweetened milk
- milk1/2 cup of shredded coconut
- 1/2 cup of chop-up almonds
- 1/2 tsp almond extract
- 1/2 tsp vanilla extract
- Pinch of salt

Instructions:
1. For easier cleanup, use parchment paper to line an 8x8-inch square baking pan.
2. Melt the sweetened condensed milk and chocolate chips together in a microwave-safe bowl. Melt in microwave at 30 second intervals, stirring between, up to smooth.
3. Combine in some salt, a dash of vanilla extract, some almond extract, and some chop-up coconut.
4. Distribute the ingredients evenly in the prepared pan.
5. Let at least 2 hrs in the fridge to set.
6. Once the fudge has set, you can use the overhanging parchment paper to take out it from the pan. Reduce to 16 equal squares.

Nutrition (per serving, approximate):
Cals: 220, Fat: 11g

Carbs: 27g

Protein: 3g

56. Caramel Macchiato Fudge

Prep Time: 15 mins

Cook Time: 10 mins

Total Time: 25 mins

Servings: 16 squares

Ingredients:

- 2 cups of white chocolate chips
- A 14-oz can of condensed milk that has been sweetened
- 1/4 cup of instant coffee granules
- 1/4 cup of caramel sauce
- 1 tsp vanilla extract
- Pinch of salt

Instructions:

1. For easier cleanup, use parchment paper to line an 8x8-inch square baking pan.
2. White chocolate chips and sweetened condensed milk Must be combined in a microwave-safe bowl. Melt in microwave at 30 second intervals, stirring between, up to smooth.
3. Add the instant coffee granules that have been dissolved in 2 tsp of hot water. Combine in the vanilla extract, a bit of salt, and caramel sauce.
4. Distribute the ingredients evenly in the prepared pan.
5. Let at least 2 hrs in the fridge to set.
6. Once the fudge has set, you can use the overhanging parchment paper to take out it from the pan. Reduce to 16 equal squares.

Nutrition (per serving, approximate):

Cals: 230, Fat: 10g

Carbs: 32g

Protein: 3g

57. Pineapple Coconut Fudge

Prep Time: 15 mins

Cook Time: 10 mins

Total Time: 25 mins

Servings: 16 pieces

Ingredients:

- 2 cups of white chocolate chips
- 1 (14-oz) can sweetened condensed milk
- 1 cup of shredded coconut
- 1/2 cup of dried pineapple, lightly chop-up
- 1 tsp vanilla extract
- A pinch of salt

Instructions:

1. Prepare a baking sheet (8x8) with parchment paper or butter.

2. White chocolate chips and sweetened condensed milk are dilute together in a pot over low heat with constant stirring up to smooth.
3. Turn off the heat and combine in the coconut flakes, dried pineapple, vanilla, and a pinch of salt.
4. Then, evenly distribute the Mixture in the baking dish.
5. Set in the fridge for at least two hrs.
6. When ready, slice the cake into 16 squares.

NUTRITION INFO (per serving):

Cals: 215, Fat: 11g

Carbs: 26g

Protein: 3g

58. Pumpkin Pecan Fudge

Prep Time: 10 mins

Cook Time: 10 mins

Total Time: 20 mins

Servings: 20 pieces

Ingredients:

- 2 cups of white chocolate chips
- 1 (14-oz) can sweetened condensed milk
- 1/2 cup of canned pumpkin puree
- 1 tsp pumpkin pie spice
- 1 cup of chop-up pecans
- 1 tsp vanilla extract
- A pinch of salt

Instructions:

1. Prepare a baking sheet (8x8) with parchment paper or butter.
2. White chocolate chips and sweetened condensed milk are dilute together in a pot over low heat with constant stirring up to smooth.
3. Add the pumpkin puree, pumpkin pie spice, pecans, vanilla essence, and a bit of salt, and combine well.
4. Then, evenly distribute the Mixture in the baking dish.
5. Set in the fridge for at least two hrs.
6. When ready, slice the arranged dessert into 20 pieces.

NUTRITION INFO (per serving):

Cals: 175, Fat: 9g

Carbs: 20g

Protein: 3g

59. Bourbon Pecan Pie Fudge

Prep Time: 15 mins

Cook Time: 10 mins

Total Time: 25 mins

Servings: 16 pieces

Ingredients:

- 2 cups of semi-sweet chocolate chips
- A 14-oz can of condensed milk that has been sweetened
- 1/2 cup of chop-up pecans
- 2 tbsp bourbon
- 1 tsp vanilla extract
- A pinch of salt

Instructions:

1. Prepare a baking sheet (8x8) with parchment paper or butter.
2. Stirring constantly, melt the semisweet chocolate chips and sweetened condensed milk over low heat in a saucepan.
3. Add the pecans, bourbon, vanilla, and a bit of salt and stir everything together.
4. Then, evenly distribute the Mixture in the baking dish.
5. Set in the fridge for at least two hrs.
6. When ready, slice the cake into 16 squares.

NUTRITION INFO (per serving):

Cals: 220, Fat: 12g

Carbs: 25g

Protein: 3g

60. Chocolate Hazelnut Fudge

Prep Time: 15 mins

Cook Time: 10 mins

Total Time: 25 mins

Servings: 20 pieces

Ingredients:

- Two cups of chocolate chips, semi-sweet
- A 14-oz can of condensed milk that has been sweetened
- 1/2 cup of chop-up hazelnuts
- 1 tsp vanilla extract
- A pinch of salt

Instructions:

1. Prepare a baking sheet (8x8) with parchment paper or butter.
2. Stirring constantly, melt the semisweet chocolate chips and sweetened condensed milk over low heat in a saucepan.
3. Add the hazelnuts, vanilla, and salt and stir to combine.
4. Then, evenly distribute the Mixture in the baking dish.
5. Set in the fridge for at least two hrs.

6. When ready, slice the arranged dessert into 20 pieces.

NUTRITION INFO (per serving):

Cals: 190, Fat: 10g

Carbs: 22g

Protein: 3g

61. Dark Chocolate Cherry Fudge

Prep Time: 15 mins

Cook Time: 5 mins

Total Time: 3 hrs 20 mins

Servings: 24 pieces

Ingredients:

- 3 cups of dark chocolate chips
- A 14-oz can of condensed milk that has been sweetened
- 1 tsp vanilla extract
- 1 cup of dried cherries

Instructions:

1. Prepare a parchment paper-lined 8x8-inch (20x20 cm) baking pan.
2. Put the dark chocolate chips and sweetened condensed milk in a microwave-safe bowl and melt it together. Stirring constantly, heat on high for 30 seconds at a time up to chocolate is completely dilute.
3. Combine in the dried cherries and vanilla extract.
4. Spread the fudge evenly in the prepared pan, then pour in the Mixture.
5. Chill for at least three hrs, or up to firm.
6. Serve by slicing into 24 pieces.

Nutrition (per serving):

Cals: 180, Fat: 8g

Carbs: 26g

Protein: 2g

62. Ginger Snap Fudge

Prep Time: 15 mins

Cook Time: 5 mins

Total Time: 3 hrs 20 mins

Servings: 24 pieces

Ingredients:

- 3 cups of white chocolate chips
- A 14-oz can of condensed milk that has been sweetened1 tsp ground ginger
- 1/2 tsp ground cinnamon
- 1/4 tsp ground cloves
- 1/4 cup of crushed gingersnap cookies

Instructions:

1. Prepare a parchment paper-lined 8x8-inch (20x20 cm) baking pan.
2. White chocolate chips and sweetened condensed milk Must be combined in a microwave-safe bowl. Stirring constantly, heat on high for 30 seconds at a time up to chocolate is completely dilute.
3. Blend in some ground ginger, some cinnamon, some cloves, and some crushed gingersnaps.
4. Spread the fudge evenly in the prepared pan, then pour in the Mixture.
5. Chill for at least three hrs, or up to firm.
6. Serve by slicing into 24 pieces.

Nutrition (per serving):

Cals: 190, Fat: 8g

Carbs: 27g, Protein: 2g

63. Almond Maple Fudge

Prep Time: 15 mins

Cook Time: 5 mins

Total Time: 3 hrs 20 mins

Servings: 24 pieces

Ingredients:

- 3 cups of white chocolate chips
- A 14-oz can of condensed milk that has been
- 1/2 cup of chop-up almonds
- 2 tbsp maple syrup
- 1/2 tsp almond extract

Instructions:

1. Prepare a parchment paper-lined 8x8-inch (20x20 cm) baking pan.
2. White chocolate chips and sweetened condensed milk Must be combined in a microwave-safe bowl. Stirring constantly, heat on high for 30 seconds at a time up to chocolate is completely dilute.
3. Combine in some almond extract, maple syrup, and chop-up almonds.
4. Spread the fudge evenly in the prepared pan, then pour in the Mixture.
5. Chill for at least three hrs, or up to firm.
6. Serve by slicing into 24 pieces.

Nutrition (per serving):

Cals: 200, Fat: 9g

Carbs: 27g

Protein: 4g

64. Chocolate Covered Pretzel Fudge

Prep Time: 15 mins

Cook Time: 5 mins

Total Time: 3 hrs 20 mins

Servings: 24 pieces

Ingredients:

- 3 cups of milk chocolate chips
- A 14-oz can of condensed milk that has been
- 1 tsp vanilla extract
- 1 cup of crushed pretzels
- 1/2 cup of semisweet chocolate chips

Instructions:

1. Prepare a parchment paper-lined 8x8-inch (20x20 cm) baking pan.
2. You can melt the milk chocolate chips and sweetened condensed milk together in the microwave. Stirring constantly, heat on high for 30 seconds at a time up to chocolate is completely dilute.
3. Combine in the crushed pretzels and vanilla extract.
4. Spread the fudge evenly in the prepared pan, then pour in the Mixture.
5. The semisweet chocolate chips Must be sprinkled on top.
6. Chill for at least three hrs, or up to firm.
7. Serve by slicing into 24 pieces.

Nutrition (per serving):

Cals: 190, Fat: 8g

Carbs: 28g

Protein: 3g

65. Cherry Chocolate Chunk Fudge

Prep Time: 15 mins

Cook Time: 10 mins

Total Time: 25 mins

Servings: 16 pieces

Ingredients:

- 3 cups of semi-sweet chocolate chips
- A 14-oz can of condensed milk that has been
- 1 tsp vanilla extract
- 1/2 cup of dried cherries
- 1/2 cup of chop-up dark chocolate chunks

Instructions:

1. Prepare a square 8x8-inch baking pan by lining it with parchment paper and leting an overhang on two opposite sides.
2. Melt the sweetened condensed milk and chocolate chips together in a microwave-safe bowl. To achieve a smooth consistency, microwave in 30-second increments while stirring after every.
3. Combine in some dried cherries, dark chocolate, and vanilla extract.

4. Spread the Mixture evenly in the pan after pouring the Mixture in.
5. Put in the fridge for at least two hrs, or up to the fudge has hardened.
6. Slice the fudge into 16 squares after removing it from the pan using the parchment paper.

Nutrition (per serving): (Approximate)
Cals: 250, Fat: 13g

Carbs: 32g

Protein: 3g

66.Toffee Almond Fudge

Prep Time: 15 mins

Cook Time: 10 mins

Total Time: 25 mins

Servings: 16 pieces

Ingredients:
- 3 cups of milk chocolate chips
- A 14-oz can of condensed milk that has been
- 1 tsp almond extract
- 1 cup of toffee bits
- 1/2 cup of chop-up almonds

Instructions:
1. Prepare a square 8x8-inch baking pan by lining it with parchment paper and leting an overhang on two opposite sides.
2. You can melt the milk chocolate chips and sweetened condensed milk together in the microwave. To achieve a smooth consistency, microwave in 30-second increments while stirring after every.
3. Almond extract, toffee bits, and chop-up almonds Must be combined and stirred in.
4. Spread the Mixture evenly in the pan after pouring the Mixture in.
5. Put in the fridge for at least two hrs, or up to the fudge has hardened.
6. Slice the fudge into 16 squares after removing it from the pan using the parchment paper.

Nutrition (per serving): (Approximate)
Cals: 280, Fat: 13g

Carbs: 36g

Protein: 4g

67.S'mores Marshmlet Fudge

Prep Time: 15 mins

Cook Time: 10 mins

Total Time: 25 mins

Servings: 16 pieces

Ingredients:
- 3 cups of milk chocolate chips
- A 14-oz can of condensed milk that has been
- 1 tsp vanilla extract
- 1 cup of mini marshmlets
- 1 cup of crushed graham crackers
- 1/2 cup of chocolate chunks

Instructions:
1. Prepare a square 8x8-inch baking pan by lining it with parchment paper and leting an overhang on two opposite sides.
2. You can melt the milk chocolate chips and sweetened condensed milk together in the microwave. To achieve a smooth consistency, microwave in 30-second increments while stirring after every.
3. Combine in the vanilla, marshmlets, graham cracker crumbs, and chocolate pieces.
4. Spread the Mixture evenly in the pan after pouring the Mixture in.
5. Put in the fridge for at least two hrs, or up to the fudge has hardened.
6. Slice the fudge into 16 squares after removing it from the pan using the parchment paper.

Nutrition (per serving): (Approximate)
Cals: 280, Fat: 13g

Carbs: 38g

Protein: 3g

68.Apple Pie Fudge

Prep Time: 15 mins

Cook Time: 10 mins

Total Time: 25 mins

Servings: 16 pieces

Ingredients:
- 3 cups of white chocolate chips
- A 14-oz can of condensed milk that has been
- 1 tsp apple pie spice
- 1 cup of dried apples, chop-up
- 1/2 cup of graham cracker crumbs

Instructions:
1. Prepare a square 8x8-inch baking pan by lining it with parchment paper and leting an overhang on two opposite sides.
2. White chocolate chips and sweetened condensed milk Must be combined in a microwave-safe bowl. To achieve a smooth consistency, microwave in 30-second increments while stirring after every.
3. Apple pie spice, dried apples, and graham cracker crumbs Must be combined and combined in.

4. Spread the Mixture evenly in the pan after pouring the Mixture in.
5. Put in the fridge for at least two hrs, or up to the fudge has hardened.
6. Slice the fudge into 16 squares after removing it from the pan using the parchment paper.

Nutrition (per serving): (Approximate)

Cals: 260, Fat: 13g

Carbs: 35g

Protein: 3.5g

69. White Chocolate Toffee Fudge

Prep Time: 15 mins

Cook Time: 5 mins

Total Time: 20 mins

Servings: 24 pieces

Ingredients:

- 3 cups of white chocolate chips
- A 14-oz can of condensed milk that has been
- 1/2 cup of toffee bits
- 1 tsp vanilla extract

Instructions:

1. Prepare a parchment paper-lined 8x8-inch (20x20 cm) baking pan.
2. White chocolate chips and sweetened condensed milk Must be combined in a microwave-safe bowl. Melt chocolate in microwave in 30-second increments, stirring between every, up to smooth.
3. Combine in the pieces of toffee and the vanilla.
4. Pour the batter into the dish and level it off.
5. Keep chilled for at least two hrs, or up to firm.
6. When ready to serve, slice into 24 pieces.

Nutrition (per serving):

Cals: 180, Fat: 8g

Carbs: 26g

Protein: 3g

70. Churro Fudge

Prep Time: 10 mins

Cook Time: 5 mins

Total Time: 15 mins

Servings: 24 pieces

Ingredients:

- 3 cups of white chocolate chips
- A 14-oz can of condensed milk that has been
- 1 tsp ground cinnamon
- 1/2 tsp vanilla extract
- 1/4 cup of granulated sugar
- 1 tsp ground cinnamon (for coating)

Instructions:

1. Prepare a parchment paper-lined 8x8-inch (20x20 cm) baking pan.
2. White chocolate chips and sweetened condensed milk Must be combined in a microwave-safe bowl. Melt chocolate in microwave in 30-second increments, stirring between every, up to smooth.
3. Combine in the vanilla extract and cinnamon.
4. Put the sugar and more cinnamon in an other bowl.
5. After the sugar and cinnamon have been combined, pour the fudge Mixture into the prepared pan.
6. Set in the fridge for at least two hrs.
7. When ready to serve, slice into 24 pieces.

Nutrition (per serving):

Cals: 160, Fat: 7g

Carbs: 23g

Protein: 2g

71. Fig and Walnut Fudge

Prep Time: 15 mins

Cook Time: 10 mins

Total Time: 25 mins

Servings: 24 pieces

Ingredients:

- 3 cups of dried figs, lightly chop-up
- 1 cup of chop-up walnuts
- A 14-oz can of condensed milk that has been
- 1/2 tsp vanilla extract

Instructions:

1. Prepare a parchment paper-lined 8x8-inch (20x20 cm) baking pan.
2. Put the dried figs and the sweetened condensed milk in a saucepan and heat through. For about 10 mins while stirring often, the sauce Must thicken enough to leave the edges of the pan.
3. Turn off the stove and add the vanilla extract and chop-up walnuts.
4. Pour the batter into the dish and level it off.
5. Set in the fridge for at least two hrs.
6. When ready to serve, slice into 24 pieces.

Nutrition (per serving):

Cals: 120, Fat: 4g

Carbs: 20g

Protein: 2g

72. Raspberry Almond Fudge

Prep Time: 15 mins

Cook Time: 5 mins

Total Time: 20 mins

Servings: 24 pieces

Ingredients:

- 3 cups of white chocolate chips
- A 14-oz can of condensed milk that has been
- 1/2 cup of freeze-dried raspberries
- 1/2 cup of chop-up almonds
- 1/2 tsp almond extract

Instructions:

1. Prepare a parchment paper-lined 8x8-inch (20x20 cm) baking pan.
2. White chocolate chips and sweetened condensed milk Must be combined in a microwave-safe bowl. Melt chocolate in microwave in 30-second increments, stirring between every, up to smooth.
3. Almond extract, almonds, and freeze-dried raspberries Must be combined together.
4. Pour the batter into the dish and level it off.
5. Set in the fridge for at least two hrs.
6. When ready to serve, slice into 24 pieces.

Nutrition (per serving):

Cals: 180, Fat: 8g

Carbs: 26g

Protein: 3g

73.Strawberry Shortcake Fudge:

Prep Time: 15 mins

Cook Time: 10 mins

Total Time: 25 mins

Servings: 24 pieces

Ingredients:

- 3 cups of white chocolate chips
- A 14-oz can of condensed milk that has been
- 1/4 cup of strawberry jam
- 1 cup of freeze-dried strawberries, crushed
- 1/2 cup of cut up shortbread cookies

Instructions:

1. Prepare a parchment paper-lined 8-by-8-inch (20-by-20-cm) square baking pan.
2. White chocolate chips and sweetened condensed milk Must be microwaved in 30-second increments, stirred between, up to smooth in a microwave-safe bowl.
3. Combine in the strawberry preserves and the freeze-dried fruit.
4. Spread the Mixture evenly in the pan after pouring the Mixture in.
5. The cut up shortbread cookies Must be sprinkled on top.

6. Set aside at least 2 hrs in the fridge.
7. Divide into squares and dig in!

Nutrition (per serving):

Cals: 200, Fat: 9g

Carbs: 27g

Protein: 2g

74.Peppermint Oreo Fudge:

Prep Time: 10 mins

Cook Time: 5 mins

Total Time: 15 mins

Servings: 36 pieces

Ingredients:

- 3 cups of semi-sweet chocolate chips
- A 14-oz can of condensed milk that has been
- 1 tsp peppermint extract
- 1 1/2 cups of crushed Oreo cookies
- 1/2 cup of crushed candy canes

Instructions:

1. Prepare a parchment paper-lined 9-by-9-inch (23-by-23-cm) baking pan.
2. Melt the chocolate chips and sweetened condensed milk in the microwave, stirring after every interval of 30 seconds, up to combined and smooth.
3. Add the peppermint extract and combine well.
4. The Oreo cookies and half the candy canes Must be cut up and added to the Mixture.
5. Spread the Mixture evenly in the pan after pouring the Mixture in.
6. The rest of the crushed candy canes Must be sprinkled on top.
7. Set aside at least 2 hrs in the fridge.
8. Divide into squares and dig in!

Nutrition (per serving):

Cals: 150, Fat: 7g

Carbs: 22g

Protein: 2g

75.Chocolate Coconut Almond Fudge:

Prep Time: 15 mins

Cook Time: 5 mins

Total Time: 20 mins

Servings: 24 pieces

Ingredients:

- 3 cups of semi-sweet chocolate chips
- A 14-oz can of condensed milk that has been
- 1 tsp vanilla extract
- 1 cup of shredded coconut
- 1/2 cup of chop-up almonds

Instructions:

1. Prepare a parchment paper-lined 8-by-8-inch (20-by-20-cm) square baking pan.
2. Melt the chocolate chips and sweetened condensed milk in the microwave, stirring after every interval of 30 seconds, up to combined and smooth.
3. Combine in the almonds, coconut, and vanilla extract.
4. Spread the Mixture evenly in the pan after pouring the Mixture in.
5. Set aside at least 2 hrs in the fridge.
6. Divide into squares and dig in!

Nutrition (per serving):

Cals: 180, Fat: 10g

Carbs: 21g

Protein: 3g

76.Maple Cinnamon Pecan Fudge:

Prep Time: 10 mins

Cook Time: 10 mins

Total Time: 20 mins

Servings: 24 pieces

Ingredients:

- 3 cups of white chocolate chips
- A 14-oz can of condensed milk that has been
- 2 tbsp maple syrup
- 1 tsp ground cinnamon
- 1 cup of chop-up pecans

Instructions:

1. Prepare a parchment paper-lined 8-by-8-inch (20-by-20-cm) square baking pan.
2. White chocolate chips and sweetened condensed milk Must be microwaved in 30-second increments, stirred between, up to smooth in a microwave-safe bowl.
3. Combine in the cinnamon and maple syrup.
4. Add the chop-up pecans and combine well.
5. Spread the Mixture evenly in the pan after pouring the Mixture in.
6. Set aside at least 2 hrs in the fridge.
7. Divide into squares and dig in!

Nutrition (per serving):

Cals: 200, Fat: 10g

Carbs: 26g

Protein: 3g

77.Caramel Banana Fudge

Prep Time: 15 mins

Cook Time: 5 mins

Total Time: 4 hrs 20 mins (including chilling time)

Servings: 16 pieces

Ingredients:

- 2 cups of semi-sweet chocolate chips
- A 14-oz can of condensed milk that has been
- 1/2 cup of ripe mashed bananas
- 1 tsp vanilla extract
- 1/2 cup of caramel sauce
- 1/2 cup of chop-up walnuts (non-compulsory)

Instructions:

1. Prepare a parchment paper-lined 8x8-inch baking tray.
2. Put the chocolate chips and sweetened condensed milk in a microwave-safe bowl and combine well. Combine well after every 30 second interval in the microwave.
3. Toss in some chop-up walnuts, some vanilla extract, and some mashed bananas.
4. Split the fudge Mixture in two and put half of it into the pan.
5. Use half of the caramel sauce and drizzle it on top.
6. Pour the remaining caramel sauce and fudge Mixture over top.
7. Stir the caramel into the fudge with a knife or toothpick.
8. Put in the fridge and chill for at least four hrs, or up to firm.
9. Divide into squares and dig in!

Nutrition (per serving):

Cals: 230, Protein: 3g

Carbs: 31g

Fat: 11g

78.Nutty Irishman Fudge

Prep Time: 15 mins

Cook Time: 5 mins

Total Time: 4 hrs 20 mins (including chilling time)

Servings: 16 pieces

Ingredients:

- 2 cups of semi-sweet chocolate chips
- A 14-oz can of condensed milk that has been
- 1/2 cup of Irish cream liqueur (e.g., Baileys)
- 1/2 cup of chop-up hazelnuts

Instructions:

1. Prepare a parchment paper-lined 8x8-inch baking tray.
2. Put the chocolate chips and sweetened condensed milk in a microwave-safe bowl and combine well. Combine well after every 30 second interval in the microwave.

3. Combine in the chop-up hazelnuts and Irish cream liqueur.
4. Spoon the fudge batter into the dish you've set aside.
5. Put in the fridge and chill for at least four hrs, or up to firm.
6. Divide into squares and dig in!

Nutrition (per serving):
Cals: 230, Protein: 3g

Carbs: 26g

Fat: 10g

79.Blueberry Cheesecake Fudge

Prep Time: 15 mins

Cook Time: 5 mins

Total Time: 4 hrs 20 mins (including chilling time)

Servings: 16 pieces

Ingredients:
- 2 cups of white chocolate chips
- A single 14-ounce can of sweetened condensed milk
- 1/2 cup of blueberry pie filling
- 1/2 cup of graham cracker crumbs
- 1 tsp vanilla extract

Instructions:
1. Prepare a parchment paper-lined 8x8-inch baking tray.
2. White chocolate chips and sweetened condensed milk Must be combined in a microwave-safe bowl. Combine well after every 30 second interval in the microwave.
3. Combine the blueberry pie filling, graham cracker crumbs, and vanilla essence in a combining bowl.
4. Spoon the fudge batter into the dish you've set aside.
5. Put in the fridge and chill for at least four hrs, or up to firm.
6. Divide into squares and dig in!

Nutrition (per serving):
Cals: 260, Protein: 3g

Carbs: 39g

Fat: 10g

80.Cinnamon Pecan Fudge

Prep Time: 15 mins

Cook Time: 5 mins

Total Time: 4 hrs 20 mins (including chilling time)

Servings: 16 pieces

Ingredients:
- 2 cups of white chocolate chips
- A 14-oz can of condensed milk that has been
- 1 tsp ground cinnamon
- 1/2 cup of chop-up pecans
- 1 tsp vanilla extract

Instructions:
1. Prepare a parchment paper-lined 8x8-inch baking tray.
2. White chocolate chips and sweetened condensed milk Must be combined in a microwave-safe bowl. Combine well after every 30 second interval in the microwave.
3. Add the vanilla extract, ground cinnamon, and chop-up pecans and stir.
4. Spoon the fudge batter into the dish you've set aside.
5. Put in the fridge and chill for at least four hrs, or up to firm.
6. Divide into squares and dig in!

Nutrition (per serving):
Cals: 270, Protein: 3g

Carbs: 35g

Fat: 12g

81.White Chocolate Apricot Fudge

Prep Time: 15 mins

Cook Time: 10 mins

Total Time: 25 mins

Servings: 24 pieces

Ingredients:
- 3 cups of white chocolate chips
- A single 14-ounce can of sweetened condensed milk
- 1 tsp vanilla extract
- 1 cup of dried apricots, chop-up
- 1/2 cup of chop-up walnuts

Instructions:
1. Prepare a square baking dish, 8 inches on a side, with parchment paper, leaving an overhang for lifting.
2. White chocolate chips and sweetened condensed milk are dilute together in a skillet over low heat, then stirred up to smooth.
3. Turn off the heat and combine in the chop-up walnuts, dried apricots, and vanilla extract.
4. Spread the Mixture evenly in the dish you have prepared.
5. Put in the fridge and chill for a minimum of 2 hrs, or up to firm.
6. Once the fudge has set, you can take out it from the dish by lifting the parchment paper.

Nutrition (per serving):
Cals: 190, Fat: 9g

Carbs: 24g

Protein: 3g

82.Cookies and Creme Fudge

Prep Time: 15 mins

Cook Time: 5 mins

Total Time: 20 mins

Servings: 24 pieces

Ingredients:

- 3 cups of white chocolate chips
- A single 14-ounce can of sweetened condensed milk
- 1 tsp vanilla extract
- 15 chocolate sandwich cookies, crushed

Instructions:

1. Prepare a parchment paper-lined 8-inch square baking dish.
2. White chocolate chips and sweetened condensed milk are dilute together in a skillet over low heat, then stirred up to smooth.
3. Bring to a boil, then turn off the heat and add the vanilla and cookie crumbs.
4. Spread the Mixture evenly in the dish after pouring the Mixture in.
5. Set aside at least 2 hrs in the fridge.
6. Prior to serving, slice into squares.

Nutrition (per serving):

Cals: 180, Fat: 8g

Carbs: 24g

Protein: 2g

83.Cranberry Eggnog Fudge

Prep Time: 10 mins

Cook Time: 10 mins

Total Time: 20 mins

Servings: 24 pieces

Ingredients:

- 3 cups of white chocolate chips
- One 14-oz can of condensed milk with added sweetness
- 1 tsp vanilla extract
- 1/2 cup of dried cranberries
- 1/2 tsp ground nutmeg

Instructions:

1. Prepare a parchment paper-lined 8-inch square baking dish.

2. White chocolate chips and sweetened condensed milk are dilute together in a skillet over low heat, then stirred up to smooth.
3. Take off the stove and combine in some ground nutmeg, some dried cranberries, and some vanilla extract.
4. Spread the Mixture evenly in the dish after pouring the Mixture in.
5. Set aside at least 2 hrs in the fridge.
6. Prior to serving, slice into squares.

Nutrition (per serving):

Cals: 190, Fat: 8g

Carbs: 28g

Protein: 2g

84.Pomegranate Pistachio Fudge

Prep Time: 15 mins

Cook Time: 10 mins

Total Time: 25 mins

Servings: 24 pieces

Ingredients:

- 3 cups of white chocolate chips
- One 14-ounce can of sweetened condensed milk
- 1 tsp vanilla extract
- 1/2 cup of shelled pistachios, chop-up
- 1/2 cup of dried pomegranate arils

Instructions:

1. Prepare a parchment paper-lined 8-inch square baking dish.
2. White chocolate chips and sweetened condensed milk are dilute together in a skillet over low heat, then stirred up to smooth.
3. After taking it off the heat, combine in the vanilla extract, pistachios, and pomegranate arils.
4. Spread the Mixture evenly in the dish after pouring the Mixture in.
5. Set aside at least 2 hrs in the fridge.
6. Prior to serving, slice into squares.

Nutrition (per serving):

Cals: 200, Fat: 9g

Carbs: 26g

Protein: 3g

85.Raspberry Lemonade Fudge

Prep Time: 15 mins

Cook Time: 10 mins

Total Time: 25 mins

Servings: 12 pieces

Ingredients:

- 2 cups of white chocolate chips

- One 14-ounce can of sweetened condensed milk
- 1/2 cup of raspberry preserves
- Zest of 1 lemon
- 1 tbsp lemon juice
- Pink food coloring (non-compulsory)

Instructions:

1. Prepare a parchment paper-lined 8x8-inch baking tray.
2. White chocolate chips and sweetened condensed milk Must be combined in a microwave-safe bowl. Stirring constantly, microwave on high for 30 second bursts up to the Mixture is dilute and smooth.
3. Combine the lemon juice, zest, and raspberry preserves in a bowl. A few drops of pink food coloring will do the trick if you're going for that hue.
4. Spread the Mixture evenly in the pan after pouring the Mixture in.
5. Set aside at least 2 hrs in the fridge.
6. Square it up and serve it.

Nutrition (per serving):

Cals: 260, Fat: 12g

Carbs: 35g

Protein: 4g

86.Toffee Brownie Fudge

Prep Time: 15 mins

Cook Time: 15 mins

Total Time: 30 mins

Servings: 16 pieces

Ingredients:

- 2 cups of semisweet chocolate chips
- One 14-oz can of condensed milk with added sweetness
- 1 cup of toffee bits
- 1 tsp vanilla extract

Instructions:

1. Prepare a parchment paper-lined 8x8-inch baking tray.
2. Put the chocolate chips and sweetened condensed milk in a microwave-safe bowl and combine well. Stirring constantly, microwave at 30-second intervals up to smooth.
3. Add the toffee pieces and vanilla and combine well.
4. Spread the Mixture evenly in the pan after pouring the Mixture in.
5. Set aside at least 2 hrs in the fridge.
6. Square it up and serve it.

Nutrition (per serving):

Cals: 250, Fat: 13g

Carbs: 32g

Protein: 3g

87.Blueberry Lemon Fudge

Prep Time: 15 mins

Cook Time: 10 mins

Total Time: 25 mins

Servings: 12 pieces

Ingredients:

- 2 cups of white chocolate chips
- One 14-ounce can of sweetened condensed milk
- 1/2 cup of blueberry preserves
- Zest of 1 lemon
- 1 tbsp lemon juice

Instructions:

1. Prepare a parchment paper-lined 8x8-inch baking tray.
2. White chocolate chips and sweetened condensed milk Must be combined in a microwave-safe bowl. Stirring constantly, microwave on high for 30 second bursts up to the Mixture is dilute and smooth.
3. Combine in the blueberry jam, lemon juice, and lemon zest.
4. Spread the Mixture evenly in the pan after pouring the Mixture in.
5. Set aside at least 2 hrs in the fridge.
6. Square it up and serve it.

Nutrition (per serving):

Cals: 260, Fat: 12g

Carbs: 35g, Protein: 4g

88.Pecan Praline Fudge

Prep Time: 15 mins

Cook Time: 15 mins

Total Time: 30 mins

Servings: 16 pieces

Ingredients:

- 2 cups of white chocolate chips
- One 14-ounce can of sweetened condensed milk
- 1 cup of chop-up pecans
- 1 tsp vanilla extract

Instructions:

1. Prepare a parchment paper-lined 8x8-inch baking tray.
2. White chocolate chips and sweetened condensed milk Must be combined in a microwave-safe bowl. Stirring constantly, microwave on high for

30 second bursts up to the Mixture is dilute and smooth.

3. Chop some pecans and some vanilla extract and combine them in.
4. Spread the Mixture evenly in the pan after pouring the Mixture in.
5. Set aside at least 2 hrs in the fridge.
6. Square it up and serve it.

Nutrition (per serving):

Cals: 270, Fat: 14g

Carbs: 35g

Protein: 4g

89.M&M Cookie Fudge

Prep Time: 15 mins

Cook Time: 10 mins

Total Time: 25 mins

Servings: 12 pieces

Ingredients:

- 2 cups of semi-sweet chocolate chips
- One 14-ounce can of sweetened condensed milk
- 1 tsp vanilla extract
- 1 cup of mini M&M's
- 1 cup of crushed chocolate cookies

Instructions:

1. Prepare a parchment paper-lined 8x8-inch baking tray.
2. Put the chocolate chips and sweetened condensed milk in a microwave-safe bowl and combine well. Stirring in between 30-second microwave bursts, continue this process up to the ingredients are thoroughly incorporated and the sauce is smooth.
3. Add the vanilla extract and combine well.
4. Mini M&Ms and smashed chocolate cookies Must be folded in carefully.
5. Spread the Mixture evenly in the pan after pouring the Mixture in.
6. Set aside at least 2 hrs in the fridge.
7. When ready, divide the set cake into 12 pieces.

90.Chocolate Malt Fudge

Prep Time: 15 mins

Cook Time: 10 mins

Total Time: 25 mins

Servings: 12 pieces

Ingredients:

- 2 cups of milk chocolate chips
- One 14-ounce can of sweetened condensed milk
- 1 tsp malted milk powder
- 1/2 cup of crushed malted milk balls

- 1/2 cup of chop-up nuts (non-compulsory)

Instructions:

1. Prepare a parchment paper-lined 8x8-inch baking tray.
2. Put the chocolate chips and sweetened condensed milk in a microwave-safe bowl and combine well. Stirring in between 30-second microwave bursts, continue this process up to the ingredients are thoroughly incorporated and the sauce is smooth.
3. Add the malted milk powder and combine it in.
4. Add the crushed malted milk balls and non-compulsory chop-up nuts and combine gently.
5. Spread the Mixture evenly in the pan after pouring the Mixture in.
6. Set aside at least 2 hrs in the fridge.
7. When ready, divide the set cake into 12 pieces.

91.White Chocolate Pistachio Cranberry Fudge

Prep Time: 15 mins

Cook Time: 10 mins

Total Time: 25 mins

Servings: 12 pieces

Ingredients:

- 2 cups of white chocolate chips
- One 14-ounce can of sweetened condensed milk
- 1/2 cup of shelled pistachios, chop-up
- 1/2 cup of dried cranberries

Instructions:

1. Prepare a parchment paper-lined 8x8-inch baking tray.
2. White chocolate chips and sweetened condensed milk Must be combined in a microwave-safe bowl. Stirring in between 30-second microwave bursts, continue this process up to the ingredients are thoroughly incorporated and the sauce is smooth.
3. Combine in the pistachios and cranberries by hand.
4. Spread the Mixture evenly in the pan after pouring the Mixture in.
5. Set aside at least 2 hrs in the fridge.
6. When ready, divide the set cake into 12 pieces.

92.Butterscotch Chocolate Swirl Fudge

Prep Time: 15 mins

Cook Time: 10 mins

Total Time: 25 mins

Servings: 12 pieces

Ingredients:

- 1 cup of butterscotch chips
- 1 cup of semi-sweet chocolate chips
- One 14-ounce can of sweetened condensed milk
- 1 tsp vanilla extract

Instructions:

1. Prepare a parchment paper-lined 8x8-inch baking tray.
2. Combine half of the sweetened condensed milk with the butterscotch chips in a microwave-safe bowl. Stirring in between 30-second microwave bursts, continue this process up to the ingredients are thoroughly incorporated and the sauce is smooth.
3. The remaining sweetened condensed milk Must be combined with the semisweet chocolate chips in a separate microwave-safe bowl. Stirring in between 30-second microwave bursts, continue this process up to the ingredients are thoroughly incorporated and the sauce is smooth.
4. The vanilla extract Must be stirred into the chocolate.
5. Dollop the butterscotch and chocolate combinees into the pan in alternating spoonfuls.
6. Marbleize the two Mixtures by gently swirling the knife between them.
7. Set aside at least 2 hrs in the fridge.
8. When ready, divide the set cake into 12 pieces.

93.Black Forest Fudge:

Prep Time: 15 mins

Cook Time: 10 mins

Total Time: 25 mins

Servings: 16 pieces

Ingredients:

- 2 cups of semisweet chocolate chips
- One 14-ounce can of sweetened condensed milk
- 1/4 cup of unsweetened cocoa powder
- 1/2 cup of chop-up maraschino cherries
- 1/2 cup of chop-up walnuts
- 1 tsp vanilla extract

Instructions:

1. Prepare a parchment paper-lined 8-inch square baking dish.
2. Stir the chocolate chips and sweetened condensed milk together in a saucepan over low heat up to smooth.
3. Add the cocoa powder and keep stirring while cooking to ensure a smooth consistency.
4. Turn off the heat and combine in the walnuts, cherries, and vanilla.

5. Evenly distribute the mixture throughout the prepared baking dish.
6. Fudge Must be chilled in the fridge for at least two hrs, or up to firm.
7. When ready, take out of the dish, let cool, and slice into squares.

NUTRITION INFO (per serving):

Cals: 232, Fat: 11g

Carbs: 31g

Protein: 4g

94.Pina Colada Fudge:

Prep Time: 15 mins

Cook Time: 10 mins

Total Time: 25 mins

Servings: 16 pieces

Ingredients:

- 2 cups of white chocolate chips
- One 14-ounce can of sweetened condensed milk
- 1/2 cup of shredded coconut
- 1/2 cup of chop-up dried pineapple
- 1 tsp coconut extract

Instructions:

1. Prepare a parchment paper-lined 8-inch square baking dish.
2. White chocolate chips and sweetened condensed milk Must be dilute together in a skillet over low heat, while constantly being stirred.
3. Combine in the dried pineapple, coconut flakes, and coconut extract.
4. Evenly distribute the mixture throughout the prepared baking dish.
5. Fudge Must be chilled in the fridge for at least two hrs, or up to firm.
6. When ready, take out of the dish, let cool, and slice into squares.

NUTRITION INFO (per serving):

Cals: 216, Fat: 10g

Carbs: 29g

Protein: 3g

95.Cappuccino Fudge:

Prep Time: 15 mins

Cook Time: 10 mins

Total Time: 25 mins

Servings: 16 pieces

Ingredients:

- 2 cups of semisweet chocolate chips
- One 14-ounce can of sweetened condensed milk
- 2 tbsp instant coffee granules

- 1 tsp vanilla extract

Instructions:
1. Prepare a parchment paper-lined 8-inch square baking dish.
2. Stir the chocolate chips and sweetened condensed milk together in a saucepan over low heat up to smooth.
3. Combine the instant coffee granules with a few tbsp of hot water, and then add them and the vanilla extract to the chocolate.
4. Distribute the mixture evenly in the baking dish.
5. Fudge Must be chilled in the fridge for at least two hrs, or up to firm.
6. When ready, take out of the dish, let cool, and slice into squares.

NUTRITION INFO (per serving):
Cals: 216, Fat: 10g

Carbs: 30g

Protein: 3g

96. White Chocolate Cherry Fudge:

Prep Time: 15 mins

Cook Time: 10 mins

Total Time: 25 mins

Servings: 16 pieces

Ingredients:
- 2 cups of white chocolate chips
- One 14-ounce can of sweetened condensed milk
- 1/2 cup of dried cherries
- 1/2 cup of chop-up macadamia nuts
- 1 tsp almond extract

Instructions:
1. Prepare a parchment paper-lined 8-inch square baking dish.
2. White chocolate chips and sweetened condensed milk Must be dilute together in a skillet over low heat, while constantly being stirred.
3. Add the almond extract, chop-up macadamia nuts, and dried cherries and combine well.
4. Evenly distribute the mixture throughout the prepared baking dish.
5. Fudge Must be chilled in the fridge for at least two hrs, or up to firm.
6. When ready, take out of the dish, let cool, and slice into squares.

NUTRITION INFO (per serving):
Cals: 237, Fat: 12g

Carbs: 29g

Protein: 4g

97. Peppermint Hot Chocolate Fudge:

Prep Time: 10 mins

Cook Time: 10 mins

Total Time: 20 mins

Servings: 16 squares

Ingredients:
- 3 cups of semi-sweet chocolate chips
- 1 can (14 ozs) sweetened condensed milk
- 1/4 cup of unsweetened cocoa powder
- 1/2 tsp peppermint extract
- 1/2 cup of crushed peppermint candies

Instructions:
1. Prepare a baking sheet that is 8 inches by 8 inches (or a similar size) by lining it with parchment paper and leaving an overhang on two opposite sides.
2. Put the chocolate chips and sweetened condensed milk in a microwave-safe bowl and combine well. Stirring after every 30 second microwave interval will ensure a smooth and dilute Mixture.
3. Add the peppermint essence and chocolate powder and combine thoroughly.
4. Spread the fudge Mixture evenly in the prepared pan.
5. Peppermint candies in their crushed form Must be sprinkled over the fudge.
6. Fudge can be leted to cool at ambient temperature up to set, or chilled to speed up the process.
7. Fudge, after firm, can be take outd from the pan by lifting the parchment paper.

Nutrition: (per serving, approximately)
Cals: 240, Fat: 11g

Carbs: 34g, Protein: 3g

98. Chocolate Pistachio Fudge:

Prep Time: 10 mins

Cook Time: 10 mins

Total Time: 20 mins

Servings: 16 squares

Ingredients:
- 3 cups of semi-sweet chocolate chips
- 1 can (14 ozs) sweetened condensed milk
- 1/2 cup of shelled pistachios, roughly chop-up
- 1 tsp vanilla extract

Instructions:
1. Prepare a baking sheet that is 8 inches by 8 inches (or a similar size) by lining it with parchment paper and leaving an overhang on two opposite sides.

2. Put the chocolate chips and sweetened condensed milk in a microwave-safe bowl and combine well. Stirring after every 30 second microwave interval will ensure a smooth and dilute Mixture.
3. Combine in the vanilla extract and chop-up pistachios.
4. Spread the fudge Mixture evenly in the prepared pan.
5. Fudge can be leted to cool at ambient temperature up to set, or chilled to speed up the process.
6. Fudge, after firm, can be take outd from the pan by lifting the parchment paper.

Nutrition: (per serving, approximately)
Cals: 280, Fat: 15g

Carbs: 34g

Protein: 5g

99.Turtle Pecan Fudge:

Prep Time: 15 mins

Cook Time: 15 mins

Total Time: 30 mins

Servings: 16 squares

Ingredients:
- 2 cups of semi-sweet chocolate chips
- 1 can (14 ozs) sweetened condensed milk
- 1 cup of chop-up pecans
- 1 tsp vanilla extract
- 1/2 cup of caramel sauce
- 1/2 cup of chocolate chips for topping
- 1/4 cup of pecan halves for topping

Instructions:
1. Prepare a baking sheet that is 8 inches by 8 inches (or a similar size) by lining it with parchment paper and leaving an overhang on two opposite sides.
2. Combine the sweetened condensed milk and the two cups of chocolate chips in a microwave-safe bowl. Stirring after every 30 second microwave interval will ensure a smooth and dilute Mixture.
3. Chop some pecans and some vanilla extract and combine them in.
4. Spread half of the fudge Mixture evenly in the prepared pan.
5. Swirl the fudge with a toothpick or knife after half the caramel sauce has been drizzled on top.
6. Spread the remaining fudge Mixture over the pan.
7. Swirl the dish one more, and drizzle the remaining caramel sauce on top.

8. Spread the remaining chocolate chips and pecan halves (half a cup of's worth) on top.
9. Fudge can be leted to cool at ambient temperature up to set, or chilled to speed up the process.
10. Fudge, after firm, can be take outd from the pan by lifting the parchment paper.

Nutrition: (per serving, approximately)
Cals: 290, Fat: 16g

Carbs: 34g

Protein: 4g

100.Chocolate Cherry Cordial Fudge:

Prep Time: 15 mins

Cook Time: 10 mins

Total Time: 25 mins

Servings: 16 squares

Ingredients:
- 2 cups of semi-sweet chocolate chips
- 1 can (14 ozs) sweetened condensed milk
- 1 cup of dried cherries, chop-up
- 1 tsp cherry extract
- 1/2 cup of chocolate chips for topping
- 1/4 cup of white chocolate chips for topping

Instructions:
1. Prepare a baking sheet that is 8 inches by 8 inches (or a similar size) by lining it with parchment paper and leaving an overhang on two opposite sides.
2. Combine the sweetened condensed milk and the two cups of chocolate chips in a microwave-safe bowl. Stirring after every 30 second microwave interval will ensure a smooth and dilute Mixture.
3. Add the cherry essence and dried cherry pieces and combine well.
4. Spread the fudge Mixture evenly in the prepared pan.
5. Add the white chocolate chips and chocolate chips, 1/2 cup of every.
6. Fudge can be leted to cool at ambient temperature up to set, or chilled to speed up the process.
7. Fudge, after firm, can be take outd from the pan by lifting the parchment paper.

Nutrition: (per serving, approximately)
Cals: 280, Fat: 13g

Carbs: 39g

Protein: 3g

101.Black and White Fudge

Prep Time: 15 mins

Cook Time: 10 mins

Total Time: 25 mins

Servings: 16 pieces

Ingredients:

- 2 cups of semisweet chocolate chips
- 1 can (14 ozs) sweetened condensed milk
- 2 cups of white chocolate chips
- 1 tsp vanilla extract

Instructions:

1. Prepare a parchment paper-lined 8x8-inch baking tray.
2. Put the semisweet chocolate chips and half the sweetened condensed milk in a microwave-safe bowl and combine well. Combine well after every 30 second interval in the microwave.
3. Spread the semisweet chocolate Mixture evenly in the pan. To set, chill in the fridge for 10 mins.
4. White chocolate chips and the remaining sweetened condensed milk Must be combined in a separate microwave-safe bowl. Heat in microwave, then whisk up to smooth. Blend in the vanilla extract.
5. Once the semisweet chocolate has set in the pan, pour the white chocolate Mixture on top. Disperse it uniformly.
6. Put it in the fridge for at least two hrs, or up to it sets.
7. When ready to serve, slice into squares.

Nutrition (per serving, approximate):
Cals: 220, Fat: 10g

Carbs: 30g

Protein: 4g

102.Peanut Butter Banana Fudge

Prep Time: 15 mins

Cook Time: 5 mins

Total Time: 20 mins

Servings: 20 pieces

Ingredients:

- 1 cup of creamy peanut butter
- 1 ripe banana, mashed
- 2 cups of powdered sugar
- 1/4 cup of unsalted butter
- 1 tsp vanilla extract

Instructions:

1. Prepare a parchment paper-lined 8x8-inch baking tray.
2. Butter Must be dilute in a pot over low heat. Combine the mashed banana and peanut butter together thoroughly.

3. Take the liquid off the heat and stir in the powdered sugar and vanilla up to it is completely incorporated and smooth.
4. Spread the Mixture evenly in the pan after pouring the Mixture in.
5. Put in the fridge and chill for at least 2 hrs, or up to firm.
6. Square it up and serve it.

Nutrition (per serving, approximate):
Cals: 150, Fat: 9g, Carbs: 16g

Protein: 3g

103.Pumpkin Spice Latte Fudge

Prep Time: 10 mins

Cook Time: 10 mins

Total Time: 20 mins

Servings: 16 pieces

Ingredients:

- 2 cups of white chocolate chips
- 1 can (14 ozs) sweetened condensed milk
- 2 tsp instant coffee granules
- 1 tsp pumpkin pie spice
- 1 tsp vanilla extract

Instructions:

1. Prepare a parchment paper-lined 8x8-inch baking tray.
2. White chocolate chips and sweetened condensed milk Must be combined in a microwave-safe bowl. Combine well after every 30 second interval in the microwave.
3. Instant coffee, pumpkin pie spice, and vanilla extract Must be stirred in up to smooth.
4. Spread the Mixture evenly in the pan after pouring the Mixture in.
5. Put in the fridge and chill for at least 2 hrs, or up to firm.
6. Square it up and serve it.

Nutrition (per serving, approximate):
Cals: 200, Fat: 8g, Carbs: 28g

Protein: 4g

104.Lemon Poppy Seed Fudge

Prep Time: 15 mins

Cook Time: 10 mins

Total Time: 25 mins

Servings: 16 pieces

Ingredients:

- 2 cups of white chocolate chips
- 1 can (14 ozs) sweetened condensed milk
- Zest of 1 lemon
- 2 tbsp lemon juice

- 1 tbsp poppy seeds

Instructions:

1. Prepare a parchment paper-lined 8x8-inch baking tray.
2. White chocolate chips and sweetened condensed milk Must be combined in a microwave-safe bowl. Combine well after every 30 second interval in the microwave.
3. Combine in the poppy seeds, lemon juice, and lemon zest up to everything is evenly distributed.
4. Spread the Mixture evenly in the pan after pouring the Mixture in.
5. Put in the fridge and chill for at least 2 hrs, or up to firm.
6. Square it up and serve it.

Nutrition (per serving, approximate):

Cals: 210, Fat: 9g

Carbs: 30g

Protein: 4g

105.Hazelnut Espresso Fudge

Prep Time: 15 mins

Cook Time: 10 mins

Total Time: 25 mins

Servings: 16 pieces

Ingredients:

- 2 cups of semi-sweet chocolate chips
- 1 can (14 oz) sweetened condensed milk
- 2 tbsp instant espresso powder
- 1/2 cup of chop-up hazelnuts
- 1 tsp vanilla extract
- Pinch of salt

Instructions:

1. Prepare a square baking dish, 8 inches on a side, by lining it with parchment paper and letting it dangle over the edges.
2. Put the chocolate chips and sweetened condensed milk in a microwave-safe bowl and combine well. Stirring in between 30-second microwave bursts, continue this process up to the ingredients are thoroughly incorporated and the sauce is smooth.
3. Combine in the ground hazelnuts, instant espresso powder, vanilla extract, and salt.
4. Then, evenly distribute the Mixture in the baking dish.
5. Put in the fridge and chill for a minimum of 2 hrs, or up to firm.
6. Once the fudge has set, use the overhanging parchment paper to take out it from the dish. Slice into 16 squares.

Nutrition (Per Serving - Approximate):

Cals: 215, Fat: 11g

Carbs: 26g

Protein: 4g

106. Apple Cinnamon Fudge

Prep Time: 10 mins

Cook Time: 10 mins

Total Time: 20 mins

Servings: 24 pieces

Ingredients:

- 2 cups of white chocolate chips
- 1 can (14 oz) sweetened condensed milk
- 1 tsp ground cinnamon
- 1/2 cup of dried apple bits
- 1 tsp vanilla extract
- Pinch of salt

Instructions:

1. Prepare a parchment paper-lined 8-inch square baking dish.
2. White chocolate chips and sweetened condensed milk Must be combined in a microwave-safe bowl. Stirring in between 30-second microwave bursts, continue this process up to the Mixture is completely smooth.
3. Combine in the salt, vanilla extract, dried apple pieces, and ground cinnamon.
4. Then, evenly distribute the Mixture in the baking dish.
5. Put it in the fridge for at least two hrs, or up to it has set at room temperature.
6. Break up into 24 servings.

Nutrition (Per Serving - Approximate):

Cals: 143, Fat: 6g

Carbs: 20g

Protein: 2g

107.Salted Caramel Pretzel Fudge

Prep Time: 15 mins

Cook Time: 10 mins

Total Time: 25 mins

Servings: 16 pieces

Ingredients:

- 2 cups of semi-sweet chocolate chips
- 1 can (14 ozs) sweetened condensed milk
- 1/2 cup of caramel sauce
- 1 cup of mini pretzels, crushed
- Sea salt for sprinkling

Instructions:

1. Prepare a parchment paper-lined 8x8-inch (20x20 cm) baking pan.
2. Put the chocolate chips and sweetened condensed milk in a microwave-safe bowl. Stirring constantly, heat in 30-second increments up to dilute and smooth.
3. Divide the fudge Mixture in half and pour half of it into the pan.
4. Top the fudge with half the caramel sauce, half the cut up pretzels, and a pinch of salt.
5. Top with the remaining fudge Mixture and pour it out evenly.
6. Sprinkle the remaining pretzels and salt with the leftover caramel sauce.
7. Set in the fridge for at least two hrs. Square it up and serve it.

Nutrition (per serving):

Cals: 280, Fat: 13g

Carbs: 38g

Protein: 4g

108. Maple Bacon Pancake Fudge

Prep Time: 20 mins

Cook Time: 10 mins

Total Time: 30 mins

Servings: 16 pieces

Ingredients:

- 2 cups of white chocolate chips
- One 14-ounce can of sweetened condensed milk
- 1/4 cup of maple syrup
- 6 slices of crispy bacon, cut up
- 1/2 cup of pancake combine

Instructions:

1. Prepare a parchment paper-lined 8x8-inch (20x20 cm) baking pan.
2. White chocolate chips and sweetened condensed milk Must be combined in a microwave-safe bowl. Stirring constantly, heat in 30-second increments up to dilute and smooth.
3. Combine the pancake combine with the maple syrup by stirring the two together.
4. Combine in the bacon bits.
5. Spread the Mixture evenly in the pan after pouring the Mixture in.
6. Set in the fridge for at least two hrs. Square it up and serve it.

Nutrition (per serving):

Cals: 290, Fat: 14g

Carbs: 38g

Protein: 5g

109. Raspberry Truffle Fudge

Prep Time: 15 mins

Cook Time: 5 mins

Total Time: 20 mins

Servings: 16 pieces

Ingredients:

- 2 cups of dark chocolate chips
- 1 can (14 ozs) sweetened condensed milk
- 1 cup of fresh raspberries
- 1 tsp vanilla extract

Instructions:

1. Prepare a parchment paper-lined 8x8-inch (20x20 cm) baking pan.
2. Dark chocolate chips and sweetened condensed milk Must be combined in a microwave-safe bowl. Stirring constantly, heat in 30-second increments up to dilute and smooth.
3. Toss in some fresh raspberries and some vanilla extract.
4. Spread the Mixture evenly in the pan after pouring the Mixture in.
5. Set in the fridge for at least two hrs. Square it up and serve it.

Nutrition (per serving):

Cals: 250, Fat: 12g

Carbs: 32g

Protein: 3g

110. Chocolate Marshmlet Swirl Fudge

Prep Time: 15 mins

Cook Time: 10 mins

Total Time: 25 mins

Servings: 16 pieces

Ingredients:

- 2 cups of semi-sweet chocolate chips
- 1 can (14 ozs) sweetened condensed milk
- 1 tsp vanilla extract
- 2 cups of mini marshmlets

Instructions:

1. Prepare a parchment paper-lined 8x8-inch (20x20 cm) baking pan.
2. Put the chocolate chips and sweetened condensed milk in a microwave-safe bowl. Stirring constantly, heat in 30-second increments up to dilute and smooth.
3. Add the vanilla extract and the mini marshmlets and stir to combine.
4. Spread the Mixture evenly in the pan after pouring the Mixture in.

5. Set in the fridge for at least two hrs. Square it up and serve it.

Nutrition (per serving):

Cals: 220, Fat: 10g

Carbs: 32g

Protein: 2g

111. Blueberry Almond Fudge

Prep Time: 15 mins

Cook Time: 5 mins

Total Time: 2 hrs 20 mins

Servings: 16 pieces

Ingredients:

- 2 cups of white chocolate chips
- 1 can of sweetened condensed milk (14 ounces)
- 1 cup of dried blueberries
- 1/2 cup of chop-up almonds
- 1 tsp almond extract
- A pinch of salt

Instructions:

1. Put some parchment paper in an 8x8-inch (20x20 cm) square baking pan and leave some overhang for lifting.
2. Melt white chocolate chips and sweetened condensed milk in a microwave-safe bowl, stirring after every 30 seconds.
3. Combine in the chop-up almonds, almond extract, and a touch of salt along with the dried blueberries.
4. Spread the Mixture evenly in the pan after pouring the Mixture in.
5. Set aside at least 2 hrs in the fridge.
6. Slice the fudge into 16 pieces, then use the overhanging parchment paper to lift it out of the pan.

NUTRITION INFO (per piece):

Cals: 200, Fat: 9g

Carbs: 28g

Protein: 3g

112. White Chocolate Strawberry Fudge

Prep Time: 15 mins

Cook Time: 5 mins

Total Time: 2 hrs 20 mins

Servings: 16 pieces

Ingredients:

- 2 cups of white chocolate chips
- One 14-ounce can of sweetened condensed milk
- 1 cup of freeze-dried strawberries, crushed
- 1 tsp vanilla extract

- A pinch of salt

Instructions:

1. Use the same directions as for the Blueberry Almond Fudge, except instead of freeze-drying the strawberries and vanilla extract, use dried blueberries and almonds.

NUTRITION INFO (per piece):

Cals: 190, Fat: 8g

Carbs: 28g

Protein: 3g

113. Almond Joy Brownie Fudge

Prep Time: 20 mins

Cook Time: 10 mins

Total Time: 3 hrs

Servings: 16 pieces

Ingredients:

- 2 cups of semi-sweet chocolate chips
- 1 can of sweetened condensed milk (14 ounces)
- 1 cup of shredded coconut
- 1/2 cup of chop-up almonds
- 1 tsp almond extract
- A pinch of salt

Instructions:

1. Semi-sweet chocolate chips, coconut shreds, chop-up almonds, almond extract, and a dash of salt are used in a recipe similar to Blueberry Almond Fudge.

NUTRITION INFO (per piece):

Cals: 220, Fat: 12g

Carbs: 26g

Protein: 3g

114. Banana Nut Bread Fudge

Prep Time: 15 mins

Cook Time: 5 mins

Total Time: 2 hrs 20 mins

Servings: 16 pieces

Ingredients:

- 2 cups of white chocolate chips
- 1 can of sweetened condensed milk (14 ounces)
- 1 ripe banana, mashed
- 1/2 cup of chop-up walnuts
- 1 tsp banana extract (non-compulsory)
- A pinch of salt

Instructions:

2. Instead of using blueberries and almonds, you can make this fudge with mashed ripe bananas, chop-up walnuts, and banana extract (if you like).

NUTRITION INFO (per piece):

Cals: 210, Fat: 10g

Carbs: 27g

Protein: 3.5g

115.Mint Oreo Cookie Fudge

Prep Time: 15 mins

Cook Time: 10 mins

Total Time: 25 mins

Servings: 16 pieces

Ingredients:

- 3 cups of (18 oz) semi-sweet chocolate chips
- 1 can of sweetened condensed milk (14 ounces)
- 2 tbsp unsalted butter
- 1 tsp peppermint extract
- 10-12 Oreo cookies, coarsely crushed

Instructions:

3. Prepare a square 8x8-inch baking pan by lining it with parchment paper and letting it dangle over the edges.
4. Melt the butter and sweetened condensed milk with the chocolate chips in a medium saucepan over low heat. Continue stirring up to all of the ingredients have dilute together smoothly.
5. Turn off the heat and add the peppermint extract to the pan.
6. Crush some Oreos and fold them in gently.
7. Spread the fudge Mixture evenly in the prepared pan.
8. Set aside at least 2 hrs in the fridge, or up to the fudge is hard.
9. Once the fudge has set, you can use the overhanging parchment paper to take out it from the pan. Slice it into 16 even pieces by laying it out on a Cutting board.
10. Prepare and savor!

NUTRITION INFO (per serving):

Cals: 280, Fat: 13g, Saturated Fat: 7g

Cholesterol: 12mg

Sodium: 77mg, Carbs: 38g

Sugar: 31g, Protein: 3g

116.Coconut Chocolate Swirl Fudge

Prep Time: 15 mins

Cook Time: 5 mins

Total Time: 3 hrs (including chilling time)

Servings: 24 pieces

Ingredients:

- 2 cups of semisweet chocolate chips
- 1 can of sweetened condensed milk (14 ounces)
- 2 tbsp unsalted butter
- 1 tsp vanilla extract
- 1 cup of shredded sweetened coconut
- 1/2 cup of white chocolate chips

Instructions:

1. Prepare a square 8x8-inch baking pan by lining it with parchment paper and letting it dangle over the sides.
2. The semisweet chocolate chips, sweetened condensed milk, and butter are dilute in a saucepan over low heat with frequent stirring.
3. Combine in some vanilla extract and coconut flakes.
4. Spread the Mixture evenly in the pan after pouring the Mixture in.
5. Melt the white chocolate chips in the microwave at 20-second intervals, stirring after every, up to smooth.
6. White chocolate Must be heated and then drizzled over the fudge in the pan.
7. Gently slide a toothpick or skewer through the white chocolate to make a swirling design.
8. Put the dish in the fridge and let it chill for at least three hrs, or up to the fudge is firm.
9. Slice into 24 pieces and use the overhanging parchment paper to lift out of the pan.

Nutrition (per serving, approximate):

Cals: 165, Fat: 8g

Carbs: 22g

Protein: 2g

117. Almond Joy Cheesecake Fudge

Prep Time: 20 mins

Cook Time: 5 mins

Total Time: 3 hrs (including chilling time)

Servings: 24 pieces

Ingredients:

- 2 cups of semisweet chocolate chips
- 1 can of sweetened condensed milk (14 ounces)
- 2 tbsp unsalted butter
- 1 tsp vanilla extract
- 1/2 cup of sweetened shredded coconut
- 1/2 cup of chop-up almonds
- 1/2 cup of milk chocolate chips

Instructions:

1. Prepare in the same way as directed for the Coconut Chocolate Swirl Fudge, substituting sweetened coconut and chop-up almonds for the white chocolate and raspberry. Refrigerate, slice, and savor.

Nutrition (per serving, approximate):

Cals: 170, Fat: 9g

Carbs: 21g

Protein: 3g

118. Chocolate Raspberry Cheesecake Fudge

Prep Time: 20 mins

Cook Time: 5 mins

Total Time: 3 hrs (including chilling time)

Servings: 24 pieces

Ingredients:

- 2 cups of white chocolate chips
- 1 can (14 ozs) sweetened condensed milk
- 2 tbsp unsalted butter
- 1 tsp vanilla extract
- 1/2 cup of freeze-dried raspberries, crushed
- 1/2 cup of semisweet chocolate chips

Instructions:

2. Use white chocolate, freeze-dried raspberries, and semisweet chocolate chips in place of the semisweet chocolate, coconut, and white chocolate in the Coconut Chocolate Swirl Fudge recipe. Cool, chop, and savor!

Nutrition (per serving, approximate):

Cals: 160, Fat: 8g

Carbs: 22g

Protein: 2g

119. Irish Cream Coffee Fudge

Prep Time: 15 mins

Cook Time: 5 mins

Total Time: 3 hrs (including chilling time)

Servings: 24 pieces

Ingredients:

- 2 cups of semisweet chocolate chips
- 1 can of sweetened condensed milk (14 ounces)
- 2 tbsp unsalted butter
- 1 tsp instant coffee granules
- 2 tbsp Irish cream liqueur (e.g., Baileys)
- 1/2 tsp vanilla extract

Instructions:

1. Proceed as directed in the Coconut Chocolate Swirl Fudge recipe, except add the Irish cream liqueur, vanilla essence, and instant coffee granules to the batter. Cool, chop, and savor!

Nutrition (per serving, approximate):

Cals: 150, Fat: 7g

Carbs: 21g

Protein: 2g

120. Dark Chocolate Mint Fudge:

Prep Time: 15 mins

Cook Time: 5 mins

Total Time: 3 hrs

Servings: About 24 pieces

Ingredients:

- 3 cups of dark chocolate chips
- 1 can of sweetened condensed milk (14 ounces)
- 1/4 cup of unsalted butter
- 1 tsp peppermint extract
- 1/2 cup of crushed peppermint candies

Instructions:

3. Press parchment paper into an 8x8-inch (or comparable) square baking dish, leting a mini overhang for simple removal.
4. Melt the butter, sweetened condensed milk, and dark chocolate chips in a saucepan over low heat, stirring all the time up to smooth.
5. Take off the heat and combine in the extract of peppermint.
6. Smooth the top of the Mixture once it has been poured into the baking dish.
7. Crushed peppermint candies Must be sprinkled on top.
8. Chill for approximately three hrs or up to solid.
9. Using the overhanging parchment paper, carefully lift the fudge out of the dish and slice it into pieces.

Nutrition (Approximate per serving):

Cals: 180, Fat: 9g

Carbs: 25g

Protein: 2g

121. S'mores Marshmlet Swirl Fudge:

Prep Time: 20 mins

Cook Time: 5 mins

Total Time: 2 hrs

Servings: About 24 pieces

Ingredients:

- 3 cups of milk chocolate chips
- 1 can of sweetened condensed milk (14 ounces)
- 1/4 cup of unsalted butter
- 1 cup of mini marshmlets
- 1 cup of crushed graham crackers
- 1/2 cup of semi-sweet chocolate chips

Instructions:

1. Proceed as directed for the Dark Chocolate Mint Fudge, except substitute the marshmlets, graham

crackers, and semi-sweet chocolate chips for the peppermint essence and candies.

Nutrition (Approximate per serving):
Cals: 200, Fat: 9g

Carbs: 28g

Protein: 2g

122.Peanut Butter and Jelly Swirl Fudge:

Prep Time: 15 mins

Cook Time: 5 mins

Total Time: 2 hrs

Servings: About 24 pieces

Ingredients:
- 3 cups of white chocolate chips
- 1 can of sweetened condensed milk (14 ounces)
- 1/4 cup of unsalted butter
- 1/2 cup of smooth peanut butter
- 1/4 cup of fruit preserves (strawberry, raspberry, or your choice)

Instructions:
1. Just before chilling, stir in the peanut butter and fruit preserves on top of the fudge Mixture, following the same directions as for the Dark Chocolate Mint Fudge.

Nutrition (Approximate per serving):
Cals: 220, Fat: 11g

Carbs: 29g

Protein: 4g

123.Hazelnut Cherry Fudge:

Prep Time: 15 mins

Cook Time: 5 mins

Total Time: 3 hrs

Servings: About 24 pieces

Ingredients:
- 3 cups of semisweet chocolate chips
- 1 can of sweetened condensed milk (14 ounces)
- 1/4 cup of unsalted butter
- 1/2 cup of chop-up hazelnuts
- 1/2 cup of dried cherries

Instructions:
1. Just before putting the fudge Mixture in the refrigerator, fold in the chop-up hazelnuts and dried cherries using the same method as for the Dark Chocolate Mint Fudge.

Nutrition (Approximate per serving):
Cals: 190, Fat: 9g

Carbs: 25g

Protein: 3g

124.Almond Raspberry Swirl Fudge

Prep Time: 20 mins

Cook Time: 5 mins

Total Time: 25 mins

Servings: 16 pieces

Ingredients:
- 2 cups of white chocolate chips
- 1 can (14 ozs) sweetened condensed milk
- 1 tsp almond extract
- 1/2 cup of slivered almonds
- 1/2 cup of raspberry preserves

Instructions:
2. Press parchment paper into an 8 × 8-inch (20 x 20 cm) square baking pan, leting a mini overhang for simple removal.
3. Combine sweetened condensed milk and white chocolate chips in a microwave-safe bowl. Microwave, stirring every 30 seconds, up to smooth and completely dilute.
4. Add the slivered almonds and almond essence and stir.
5. Evenly distribute half of the fudge Mixture into the pan that has been prepared.
6. To make swirling the raspberry preserves easier, microwave them for a brief period of time. Spoonfuls of raspberry preserves Must be dropped onto the pan of fudge.
7. Place the remaining fudge Mixture on top and swirl the raspberry preserves through the fudge with a knife or skewer.
8. Chill the fudge for a minimum of two hrs or up to it solidifies.
9. After the fudge has hardened, take out it from the pan using the overhanging parchment paper and slice it into squares.

NUTRITION INFO (per serving, approximate):
Cals: 240, Fat: 10g

Carbs: 34g

Protein: 4g

125.Ginger Lemon Fudge

Prep Time: 15 mins

Cook Time: 5 mins

Total Time: 20 mins

Servings: 20 pieces

Ingredients:
- 2 cups of white chocolate chips
- 1 can (14 ozs) sweetened condensed milk
- 1 tbsp finely grated lemon zest
- 1 tbsp finely grated fresh ginger

- Yellow food coloring (non-compulsory)

Instructions:
1. Press parchment paper into an 8 × 8-inch (20 x 20 cm) square baking pan, leting a mini overhang for simple removal.
2. Combine sweetened condensed milk and white chocolate chips in a microwave-safe bowl. Microwave, stirring every 30 seconds, up to smooth and completely dilute.
3. Add the fresh ginger and finely grated lemon zest and stir. If you would like a more vivid color, add a few drops of yellow food coloring.
4. Transfer the fudge Mixture into the pan that has been ready and level it out.
5. Chill the fudge for a minimum of two hrs or up to it solidifies.
6. After the fudge has hardened, take out it from the pan using the overhanging parchment paper and slice it into squares.

NUTRITION INFO (per serving, approximate):
Cals: 160, Fat: 6g

Carbs: 24g

Protein: 2g

126. Espresso Chocolate Swirl Fudge

Prep Time: 20 mins

Cook Time: 5 mins

Total Time: 25 mins

Servings: 16 pieces

Ingredients:
- 2 cups of semi-sweet chocolate chips
- 1 can (14 ozs) sweetened condensed milk
- 2 tbsp instant espresso powder
- 1/2 cup of white chocolate chips

Instructions:
1. Press parchment paper into an 8 × 8-inch (20 x 20 cm) square baking pan, leting a mini overhang for simple removal.
2. Sweetened condensed milk and semi-sweet chocolate chips Must be combined in a microwave-safe bowl. Microwave, stirring every 30 seconds, up to smooth and completely dilute.
3. Add the instant espresso powder to the fudge Mixture after dissolving it in a tbsp of boiling water.
4. Transfer the fudge Mixture into the pan that has been ready and level it out.
5. Pour the dilute white chocolate chips onto the fudge.
6. Swirl the white chocolate into the fudge using a knife or skewer.

7. Chill the fudge for a minimum of two hrs or up to it solidifies.
8. After the fudge has hardened, take out it from the pan using the overhanging parchment paper and slice it into squares.

NUTRITION INFO (per serving, approximate):
Cals: 210, Fat: 11g

Carbs: 30g

Protein: 2g

127. Eggnog Cookie Fudge

Prep Time: 20 mins

Cook Time: 5 mins

Total Time: 25 mins

Servings: 16 pieces

Ingredients:
- 2 cups of white chocolate chips
- 1 can (14 ozs) sweetened condensed milk
- 1 tsp nutmeg
- 1 tsp vanilla extract
- 1 cup of crushed gingerbread or gingersnap cookies

Instructions:
1. Press parchment paper into an 8 × 8-inch (20 x 20 cm) square baking pan, leting a mini overhang for simple removal.
2. Combine sweetened condensed milk and white chocolate chips in a microwave-safe bowl. Microwave, stirring every 30 seconds, up to smooth and completely dilute.
3. Combine in vanilla extract and nutmeg.
4. Add the crushed gingersnap or gingerbread cookies and combine well.
5. Transfer the fudge Mixture into the pan that has been ready and level it out.
6. Chill the fudge for a minimum of two hrs or up to it solidifies.
7. After the fudge has hardened, take out it from the pan using the overhanging parchment paper and slice it into squares.

NUTRITION INFO (per serving, approximate):
Cals: 220, Fat: 9g

Carbs: 32g

Protein: 3g

128.Almond Cherry Fudge

Prep Time: 15 mins

Cook Time: 10 mins

Total Time: 25 mins

Servings: 16 pieces

Ingredients:

- 2 cups of semi-sweet chocolate chips
- 1 can of sweetened condensed milk (14 ounces)
- 1 tsp almond extract
- 1/2 cup of chop-up almonds
- 1/2 cup of dried cherries

Instructions:

1. Leaving an overhang on the sides, line an 8 × 8-inch square baking pan with parchment paper.
2. Stir together the chocolate chips and sweetened condensed milk in a medium saucepan over low heat. Once the chocolate has dilute completely and the Mixture is smooth, stir.
3. Take off the heat and combine in the dried cherries, chop-up almonds, and almond extract.
4. Transfer the blend into the ready pan and level it out.
5. Chill the fudge for a minimum of two hrs or up to it solidifies.
6. Using the overhanging parchment paper, carefully take out the fudge from the pan and slice it into 16 pieces.

NUTRITION INFO (per serving):

Cals: 226, Fat: 11g

Carbs: 31g

Protein: 4g

129. Cranberry White Chocolate Swirl Fudge

Prep Time: 15 mins

Cook Time: 10 mins

Total Time: 25 mins

Servings: 16 pieces

Ingredients:

- 2 cups of white chocolate chips
- 1 can of sweetened condensed milk (14 ounces)
- 1 tsp vanilla extract
- 1/2 cup of dried cranberries

Instructions:

1. Use white chocolate chips and dried cranberries in place of the components specified in Almond Cherry Fudge, then follow the same methods.

NUTRITION INFO (per serving):

Cals: 246, Fat: 12g

Carbs: 35g

Protein: 3g

130. Chocolate Hazelnut Swirl Fudge

Prep Time: 15 mins

Cook Time: 10 mins

Total Time: 25 mins

Servings: 16 pieces

Ingredients:

- 2 cups of semi-sweet chocolate chips
- 1 can of sweetened condensed milk (14 ounces)
- 1 tsp hazelnut extract
- 1/2 cup of chop-up hazelnuts

Instructions:

1. Use hazelnut essence and chop-up hazelnuts in place of the ingredients specified in Almond Cherry Fudge, and proceed as directed.

NUTRITION INFO (per serving):

Cals: 232, Fat: 11g

Carbs: 31g

Protein: 4g

131. Chocolate Pistachio Raspberry Fudge

Prep Time: 15 mins

Cook Time: 10 mins

Total Time: 25 mins

Servings: 16 pieces

Ingredients:

- 2 cups of semi-sweet chocolate chips
- 1 can of sweetened condensed milk (14 ounces)
- 1 tsp raspberry extract
- 1/2 cup of chop-up pistachios

Instructions:

1. Use chop-up pistachios and raspberry extract in place of the ingredients specified in Almond Cherry Fudge, then proceed as directed.

NUTRITION INFO (per serving):

Cals: 231, Fat: 11g

Carbs: 31g

Protein: 4g

132. Tiramisu Cheesecake Fudge

Prep Time: 20 mins

Cook Time: 10 mins

Total Time: 30 mins

Servings: About 24 pieces

Ingredients:

- 2 cups of semi-sweet chocolate chips
- 1 can of sweetened condensed milk (14 ounces)
- 1 tsp instant coffee granules
- 1 cup of crushed ladyfingers or shortbread cookies
- 1 cup of mascarpone cheese
- 1 tsp vanilla extract

- Cocoa powder for dusting

Instructions:

2. Press parchment paper into an 8 × 8-inch square baking dish, leting a mini overhang for simple removal.
3. Place the chocolate chips and sweetened condensed milk in a bowl that is suitable to use in the microwave. Cook, stirring, in 30-second bursts in the microwave up to well combined and dilute.
4. Add the instant coffee granules to the chocolate Mixture after dissolving them in 1 tbsp of hot water. Combine thoroughly.
5. Add the vanilla extract, mascarpone cheese, and crushed cookies and stir up to well blended.
6. Smooth the top of the baked dish after adding the fudge Mixture.
7. Place in the refrigerator up to the fudge solidifies, preferably 4 hrs.
8. After the fudge has hardened, take it out of the plate, sprinkle some cocoa powder on top, and slice it into squares.

NUTRITION INFO (Per Serving):

Cals: 180, Fat: 10g

Carbs: 20g

Protein: 2g

133. Salted Caramel Apple Pie Fudge

Prep Time: 15 mins

Cook Time: 10 mins

Total Time: 25 mins

Servings: About 24 pieces

Ingredients:

- 2 cups of white chocolate chips
- 1 can of sweetened condensed milk (14 ounces)
- 1/2 cup of unsweetened applesauce
- 1/2 tsp cinnamon
- 1/4 tsp salt
- 1/4 cup of caramel sauce
- Sea salt for sprinkling

Instructions:

9. Press parchment paper into an 8 × 8-inch square baking dish, leting a mini overhang for simple removal.
10. Place the white chocolate chips and sweetened condensed milk in a bowl that is safe to use in the microwave. Cook, stirring, in 30-second bursts in the microwave up to well combined and dilute.
11. Add the salt, cinnamon, and applesauce and stir up to thoroughly combined.
12. Smooth the top of the prepared dish after adding half of the fudge Mixture to it.

13. Pour the remaining fudge Mixture over the caramel sauce-drizzled fudge.
14. To swirl the caramel sauce through the fudge, use a toothpick or a knife.
15. Add a dash of sea salt.
16. Place in the refrigerator up to the fudge solidifies, preferably 4 hrs.
17. After the fudge solidifies, take it off of the plate and slice it into squares.

NUTRITION INFO (Per Serving):

Cals: 150, Fat: 7g

Carbs: 22g

Protein: 2g

134. Cinnamon Roll Cheesecake Fudge

Prep Time: 15 mins

Cook Time: 10 mins

Total Time: 25 mins

Servings: About 24 pieces

Ingredients:

- 2 cups of white chocolate chips
- 1 can of sweetened condensed milk (14 ounces)
- 1 tsp ground cinnamon
- 1/2 cup of cream cheese, melted
- 1 tsp vanilla extract
- Cinnamon sugar for dusting

Instructions:

1. Press parchment paper into an 8 × 8-inch square baking dish, leting a mini overhang for simple removal.
2. Place the white chocolate chips and sweetened condensed milk in a bowl that is safe to use in the microwave. Cook, stirring, in 30-second bursts in the microwave up to well combined and dilute.
3. Add the melted cream cheese, ground cinnamon, and vanilla essence; stir up to thoroughly blended.
4. Smooth the top of the baked dish after adding the fudge Mixture.
5. Add a dash of cinnamon sugar.
6. Place in the refrigerator up to the fudge solidifies, preferably 4 hrs.
7. After the fudge has hardened, take it out of the plate and slice it into squares.

NUTRITION INFO (Per Serving):

Cals: 160, Fat: 8g

Carbs: 20g

Protein: 2g

135. Pecan Pie Cheesecake Fudge

Prep Time: 20 mins

Cook Time: 10 mins

Total Time: 30 mins

Servings: About 24 pieces

Ingredients:

- 2 cups of milk chocolate chips
- 1 can of sweetened condensed milk (14 ounces)
- 1/2 cup of chop-up pecans
- 1/4 cup of cream cheese, melted
- 1 tsp vanilla extract
- 1/4 tsp salt

Instructions:

1. Press parchment paper into an 8 × 8-inch square baking dish, leting a mini overhang for simple removal.
2. Place the milk chocolate chips and sweetened condensed milk in a bowl that is suitable to use in the microwave. Cook, stirring, in 30-second bursts in the microwave up to well combined and dilute.
3. Add the melted cream cheese, chop-up pecans, vanilla essence, and salt, and stir up to thoroughly combined.
4. Smooth the top of the baked dish after adding the fudge Mixture.
5. Place in the refrigerator up to the fudge solidifies, preferably 4 hrs.
6. After the fudge solidifies, take it off of the plate and slice it into squares.

NUTRITION INFO (Per Serving):

Cals: 160, Fat: 8g

Carbs: 19g

Protein: 2g

136. Butterscotch Pecan Cookie Fudge

Prep Time: 15 mins

Cook Time: 5 mins

Total Time: 4 hrs 20 mins

Servings: 16 pieces

Ingredients:

- 3 cups of butterscotch chips
- 1 can of sweetened condensed milk (14 ounces)
- 1/2 cup of unsalted butter
- 1 tsp vanilla extract
- 1 cup of chop-up pecans
- 1 cup of cut up shortbread cookies

Instructions:

1. Using parchment paper, line an 8 x 8-inch square baking sheet, leaving an overhang for simple removal.
2. Melt butter, sweetened condensed milk, and butterscotch chips in a medium saucepan over

low heat, stirring regularly up to smooth and well blended.
3. Take off the heat and combine in the pecans, shortbread cookie crumbs, and vanilla extract.
4. Transfer the blend into the ready pan and level it out.
5. Place in the refrigerator up to firm, at least 4 hrs.
6. Lift the fudge out of the pan using the overhanging parchment paper. Separate into 16 halves.

Nutrition (per serving):

Cals: 315, Fat: 18g

Carbs: 36g

Protein: 3g

137. Chocolate Cherry Almond Fudge

Prep Time: 15 mins

Cook Time: 5 mins

Total Time: 3 hrs 20 mins

Servings: 20 pieces

Ingredients:

- 3 cups of semisweet chocolate chips
- 1 can of sweetened condensed milk (14 ounces)
- 1/2 cup of unsalted butter
- 1 tsp almond extract
- 1 cup of dried cherries
- 1/2 cup of chop-up almonds

Instructions:

1. Using parchment paper, line an 8 x 8-inch square baking sheet, leaving an overhang for simple removal.
2. Melt the butter, sweetened condensed milk, and chocolate chips in a medium saucepan over low heat, stirring regularly up to smooth and well blended.
3. Take off the heat and combine in the chop-up almonds, dried cherries, and almond extract.
4. Transfer the blend into the ready pan and level it out.
5. Place in the fridge up to set, preferably for three hrs.
6. Lift the fudge out of the pan using the overhanging parchment paper. Divide into twenty halves.

Nutrition (per serving):

Cals: 220, Fat: 12g

Carbs: 27g

Protein: 3g

138. Pumpkin Praline Fudge

Prep Time: 10 mins

Cook Time: 5 mins

Total Time: 4 hrs 15 mins

Servings: 24 pieces

Ingredients:

- 2 cups of white chocolate chips
- 1 can of sweetened condensed milk (14 ounces)
- 1/2 cup of unsalted butter
- 1/2 cup of canned pumpkin puree
- 1 tsp pumpkin pie spice
- 1 cup of chop-up pecans
- 1 tsp vanilla extract

Instructions:

1. Using parchment paper, line an 8 x 8-inch square baking sheet, leaving an overhang for simple removal.
2. Melt butter, sweetened condensed milk, and white chocolate chips in a medium saucepan over low heat, stirring regularly up to smooth and well blended.
3. Add the pumpkin puree and pumpkin pie spice and stir up to well combined.
4. Take off the heat and combine in the vanilla extract and chop-up pecans.
5. Transfer the blend into the ready pan and level it out.
6. Place in the refrigerator up to firm, at least 4 hrs.
7. Lift the fudge out of the pan using the overhanging parchment paper. Divide into 24 halves.

Nutrition (per serving):

Cals: 180, Fat: 11g

Carbs: 20g

Protein: 2g

139. White Chocolate Almond Joy Fudge

Prep Time: 15 mins

Cook Time: 5 mins

Total Time: 3 hrs 20 mins

Servings: 16 pieces

Ingredients:

- 3 cups of white chocolate chips
- 1 can of sweetened condensed milk (14 ounces)
- 1/2 cup of unsalted butter
- 1 cup of shredded coconut
- 1 cup of chop-up almonds
- 1 tsp almond extract

Instructions:

1. Using parchment paper, line an 8 x 8-inch square baking sheet, leaving an overhang for simple removal.

2. Melt butter, sweetened condensed milk, and white chocolate chips in a medium saucepan over low heat, stirring regularly up to smooth and well blended.
3. Take off the heat and combine in the almond extract, chop-up almonds, and shredded coconut.
4. Transfer the blend into the ready pan and level it out.
5. Place in the fridge up to set, preferably for three hrs.
6. Lift the fudge out of the pan using the overhanging parchment paper. Separate into 16 halves.

Nutrition (per serving):

Cals: 285, Fat: 19g

Carbs: 26g

Protein: 4g

140. Caramel Apple Cider Fudge

Prep Time: Approximately 20 mins

Cook Time: Approximately 10 mins

Total Time: About 30 mins

Servings: 16 pieces

Ingredients:

- 2 cups of white chocolate chips
- 1 can sweetened condensed milk
- 2 tbsp butter
- 1/4 cup of caramel sauce
- 1/4 cup of apple cider reduction
- 1/2 tsp cinnamon
- 1/4 tsp nutmeg
- 1/2 cup of dried apple pieces

Instructions:

1. Using parchment paper, line an 8 x 8-inch square baking sheet.
2. Butter, sweetened condensed milk, and white chocolate chips Must all be combined in a pot. Melt slowly while stirring all the time.
3. Smoothly stir in the nutmeg, cinnamon, apple cider reduction, and caramel sauce.
4. After turning off the heat, fold in the dried apple chunks.
5. Once the pan is ready, pour the Mixture into it and chill it up to it solidifies.
6. Slice into sixteen pieces, then savor!

141. Peppermint Mocha Cheesecake Fudge

Prep Time: Approximately 20 mins

Cook Time: Approximately 10 mins

Total Time: About 30 mins

Servings: 16 pieces

Ingredients:

- 2 cups of semisweet chocolate chips
- 1 can sweetened condensed milk
- 2 tbsp butter
- 1/4 cup of cream cheese
- 1 tsp instant coffee granules
- 1/4 cup of crushed peppermint candies

Instructions:

1. Using parchment paper, line an 8 x 8-inch square baking sheet.
2. Butter, sweetened condensed milk, and chocolate chips Must all be combined in a pot. Melt slowly while stirring all the time.
3. Add instant coffee and cream cheese, stirring up to smooth.
4. After adding the ingredients to the pan that has been ready, cover it with crushed peppermint candy.
5. Let it set in the fridge and then slice into sixteen pieces.

142. Caramel Brownie Cheesecake Fudge

Prep Time: Approximately 20 mins

Cook Time: Approximately 10 mins

Total Time: About 30 mins

Servings: 16 pieces

Ingredients:

- 2 cups of dark chocolate chips
- 1 can sweetened condensed milk
- 2 tbsp butter
- 1/4 cup of cream cheese
- 1/4 cup of caramel sauce
- 1/2 cup of brownie chunks

Instructions:

1. Using parchment paper, line an 8 x 8-inch square baking sheet.
2. Butter, sweetened condensed milk, and dark chocolate chips Must all be combined in a pot. Melt slowly while stirring all the time.
3. Add the caramel sauce and cream cheese, stirring up to smooth.
4. Add brownie bits and fold.
5. Once the pan is ready, pour the Mixture into it and chill it up to it solidifies. Separate into 16 halves.

143. Chocolate Raspberry Truffle Fudge

Prep Time: Approximately 20 mins

Cook Time: Approximately 10 mins

Total Time: About 30 mins

Servings: 16 pieces

Ingredients:

- 2 cups of dark chocolate chips
- 1 can sweetened condensed milk
- 2 tbsp butter
- 1/4 cup of raspberry puree
- 1/4 cup of chop-up raspberries
- 1/4 tsp almond extract

Instructions:

1. Using parchment paper, line an 8 x 8-inch square baking sheet.
2. Butter, sweetened condensed milk, and dark chocolate chips Must all be combined in a pot. Melt slowly while stirring all the time.
3. Add almond extract and raspberry puree, stirring up to smooth.
4. Add chop-up raspberries and fold.
5. Once the pan is ready, pour the Mixture into it and chill it up to it solidifies. Separate into 16 halves.

144. Gingerbread Cheesecake Fudge

Prep Time: 15 mins

Cook Time: 5 mins

Total Time: 3 hrs 20 mins

Servings: 16 squares

Ingredients:

- 3 cups of white chocolate chips
- 1 can of sweetened condensed milk (14 ounces)
- 1/4 cup of unsalted butter
- 1 tsp ground ginger
- 1 tsp ground cinnamon
- 1/2 tsp ground nutmeg
- 1/4 tsp ground cloves
- 1/2 cup of graham cracker crumbs
- 8 ozs cream cheese, melted
- 1 tsp vanilla extract

Instructions:

1. Using parchment paper, line an 8 × 8-inch square baking dish, leaving an overhang on two edges for ease of removal.
2. Put the butter, sweetened condensed milk, and white chocolate chips in a bowl that is safe to microwave. Microwave the Mixture for 30 second bursts, stirring in between, up to it's smooth and completely dilute.
3. Add the ground cloves, ground nutmeg, ground cinnamon, and ground ginger and stir.
4. Evenly distribute half of the Mixture into the baking dish that has been preheated. Place in the fridge and let cool for half an hr.
5. Meanwhile, get the cheesecake layer ready. Beat

the vanilla extract and melted cream cheese up to smooth in a combining dish.

6. Cover the cold layer of fudge in the baking dish with the cream cheese Mixture.
7. Over the cream cheese layer, scatter graham cracker crumbs.
8. Evenly distribute the leftover white chocolate fudge Mixture throughout the cream cheese layer as you pour it on.
9. Let the fudge to set in the fridge for a minimum of two hrs.
10. After it sets, take out the fudge from the baking dish by using the overhanging parchment paper. Serve after Cutting into squares.

Nutrition (per serving):
Cals: 310, Total Fat: 18g, Saturated Fat: 11g, Cholesterol: 33mg, Sodium: 123mg, Total Carbs: 35g, Sugars: 32g, Protein: 3g

145. White Chocolate Eggnog Fudge

Prep Time: 10 mins

Cook Time: 5 mins

Total Time: 2 hrs 15 mins

Servings: 24 squares

Ingredients:
- 3 cups of white chocolate chips
- 1 can of sweetened condensed milk (14 ounces)
- 1/4 cup of unsalted butter
- 1/4 cup of eggnog
- 1/4 tsp ground nutmeg
- 1 tsp vanilla extract
- Pinch of salt
- 1/2 cup of chop-up toasted pecans (non-compulsory)

Instructions:
1. Using parchment paper, line an 8 × 8-inch square baking dish, leaving an overhang on two edges for ease of removal.
2. Put the butter, sweetened condensed milk, and white chocolate chips in a bowl that is safe to microwave. Microwave the Mixture for 30 second bursts, stirring in between, up to it's smooth and completely dilute.
3. Add the ground nutmeg, vanilla extract, eggnog, and a mini amount of salt and stir.
4. Add the chop-up toasted pecans, if desired.
5. Transfer the Mixture into the baking dish that has been preheated and level it out.
6. Let the fudge to set in the fridge for a minimum of two hrs.

7. After it sets, take out the fudge from the baking dish by using the overhanging parchment paper. Serve after Cutting into squares.

Nutrition (per serving):
Cals: 173, Total Fat: 9g, Saturated Fat: 5g

Cholesterol: 13mg, Sodium: 34mg

Total Carbs: 21g

Sugars: 20g, Protein: 2g

146. Cranberry Stuffed Acorn Squash

Prep Time: 15 mins

Cook Time: 45 mins

Total Time: 1 hr

Servings: 4

Ingredients:
- 2 acorn squash, halved and seeds take outd
- 1 cup of fresh cranberries
- 1/2 cup of chop-up pecans
- 1/4 cup of brown sugar
- 2 tbsp butter, dilute
- 2 tbsp maple syrup
- 1 tsp ground cinnamon
- Salt and pepper as needed

Instructions:
1. Have a 375F (190C) oven ready.
2. Fresh cranberries, pecan pieces, brown sugar, dilute butter, maple syrup, ground cinnamon, salt, and pepper Must all be combined together in a bowl.
3. Fill the cranberry Mixture into the hollows of the acorn squash.
4. Put the aluminum foil-covered acorn squash halves in the oven.
5. Cook for 30 mins in an oven that has been preheated. Once the squash is cooked and the cranberries are bubbling, take out the foil and continue baking for 15 more mins.
6. Take out of the oven and cool for a couple of mins before serving.

Nutrition (per serving):
Cals: 280, Fat: 9g

Carbs: 53g

Fiber: 6g, Protein: 3g

147. Pecan Pie Bars

Prep Time: 15 mins

Cook Time: 45 mins

Total Time: 1 hr

Servings: 12

Ingredients:
For the Crust:

- 1 1/2 cups of all-purpose flour
- 1/2 cup of unsalted butter, cold and cubed
- 1/4 cup of granulated sugar
- 1/4 tsp salt

For the Filling:

- 3/4 cup of light corn syrup
- 1/2 cup of granulated sugar
- 1/2 cup of brown sugar
- 2 Big eggs
- 2 tbsp unsalted butter, dilute
- 1 tsp vanilla extract
- 1 1/2 cups of pecan halves

Instructions:

1. Bake at 350 Ds Fahrenheit (175 Ds Celsius) and prepare a 9 by 9 inch (23 by 23 centimeter) baking pan with parchment paper.
2. Flour, cold cubed butter, sugar, salt, and granulated sugar Must be combined in a mixer. Pulse the ingredients up to they have the texture of coarse crumbs.
3. Prepare a baking dish by pressing the crust Mixture into the bottom. If you want a light golden color, bake for 15-20 mins. Put in a separate bowl and put the oven off.
4. Combine the corn syrup, granulated sugar, brown sugar, eggs, dilute butter, and vanilla extract in a Big bowl and whisk up to smooth.
5. Add the halved pecans and combine well.
6. Cover the baked crust with the pecan filling.
7. Bake for 25 to 30 mins in the preheated oven, or up to the filling is set and a toothpick inserted in the center comes out clean.
8. Pecan pie bars are best served cold, so let them chill in the fridge for a few hrs after baking before Cutting them into squares.

Nutrition (per serving):
Cals: 350, Fat: 19g

Carbs: 43g

Fiber: 2g, Protein: 4g

148.Mexican Churros with Chocolate Sauce

Prep Time: 15 mins

Cook Time: 15 mins

Total Time: 30 mins

Servings: 4

Ingredients:
For Churros:

- 1 cup of water
- 2 tbsp white sugar

- 2 tbsp vegetable oil
- 1/2 tsp salt
- 1 cup of all-purpose flour
- 2 quarts oil for frying
- 1/2 cup of white sugar
- 1 tsp ground cinnamon

For Chocolate Sauce:

- 1/2 cup of heavy cream
- 1 cup of semisweet chocolate chips

Instructions:

1. Water, 2 tsp sugar, 2 tbsp vegetable oil, and salt Must all be combined in a pot. After bringing to a boil, turn off the heat. Add the flour and stir up to a ball forms.
2. In a deep fryer or deep pan, heat the oil for frying to 375°F (190°C). Using a pastry bag, pipe strips of dough into the hot oil.
3. Dry on paper towels after frying up to golden.
4. Combine 1/2 cup of sugar and 1/2 tsp cinnamon in a mini bowl. Drained churros are rolled with cinnamon sugar.
5. The heavy cream Must be heated up to it starts to steam in a different pan. Add the chocolate chips after turning off the heat. up to smooth, stir.
6. Warm chocolate sauce is served alongside the churros for dipping.

Nutrition (per serving):
Cals: 400, Protein: 4g, Carbs: 50g

Fat: 22g, Fiber: 2g

149.Polish Bigos (Hunter's Stew)

Prep Time: 30 mins

Cook Time: 2 hrs

Total Time: 2 hrs and 30 mins

Servings: 6

Ingredients:

- 1 lb sauerkraut
- 1 lb fresh cabbage, shredded
- 1 lb kielbasa sausage, split
- 1 lb pork Muster, diced
- 1 onion, chop-up
- 2 cloves garlic, chop-up
- 1/2 cup of dried mushrooms, soaked and chop-up
- 1 bay leaf
- 1 tsp caraway seeds
- 1 tsp marjoram
- Salt and pepper as needed

Instructions:

1. Garlic and onions Must be cooked till transparent in a big pot.

2. Brown the meat by including kielbasa and pork Muster.
3. Add mushrooms, fresh cabbage, and sauerkraut. Stir thoroughly.
4. Add salt, pepper, marjoram, a bay leaf, and caraway seeds. Completely combine.
5. Simmer for two hrs, stirring occasionally, under a cover of water.
6. Serve warm alongside crusty bread.

Nutrition (per serving):
Cals: 400, Protein: 18g, Carbs: 12g

Fat: 32g, Fiber: 6g

150. Turkish Lahmacun

Prep Time: 30 mins

Cook Time: 15 mins

Total Time: 45 mins

Servings: 4

Ingredients:
- 1 lb ground beef or lamb
- 1 onion, lightly chop-up
- 2 cloves garlic, chop-up
- 2 tomatoes, lightly chop-up
- 2 tbsp tomato paste
- 2 tbsp red pepper paste (non-compulsory)
- 1 tsp ground cumin
- 1 tsp paprika
- Salt and pepper as needed
- 1/2 cup of fresh parsley, chop-up
- 4 round flatbreads or pizza dough
- Olive oil for brushing

Instructions:
1. In Combine the ground meat with the chop-up garlic, chop-up onion, chop-up tomatoes, tomato paste, red pepper paste (if using), cumin, paprika, salt, and pepper in a sizable bowl.
2. Four equal servings of the meat combination Must be taken.
3. Set your oven's temperature to 450°F (230°C).
4. Every amount of meat Mixture Must be thinly rolled out onto a flatbread or pizza dough, leaving a thin border all around.
5. Olive oil the borders, then bake for 10 to 15 mins, or up to the meat is cooked and the edges are crispy.
6. the lahmacun with freshly chop-up parsley.
7. Serve hot and roll up.

NUTRITION INFO:
Cals: 350-400 kcal, Protein: 20-25g, Carbs: 30-35g, Fat: 15-20g

Made in the USA
Las Vegas, NV
08 December 2024

13633032R00028